I SLAY... GIANTS!!!

A SPIRITUAL & PRACTICAL APPROACH TO BREAST CANCER

Joyce L. Trotman

Dedication

This book is dedicated foremost to my sister Jocelyn, who has been by my side not only through this diagnosis as a companion but also as one of the best siblings to have ever graced this world with her presence. I also would like to acknowledge my baby sister Joy and brother Keith, who never let me sit on my dreams and aspirations whether successful or not. Special thanks and a whole lot of admiration to my mother, husband, grandmother, and the rest of my community for the loving support of my endeavors. Shout out to my spiritual family holding it down in the ATL. I love you guys, and there ain't NOTHING you can do about it.

Love, thanksgiving, and praise to the Lord Jesus Christ, who calls us to, equips us appropriately and guides us through our life's battles. Honor and glory to the Most High God and His Holy Spirit our teacher and guide.

Forward

"I Slay GIANTS!" is remarkable; yet a powerful compilation of floetry of poetry in slaying every GIANT attached to your kingdom assignment. Having the essential operational tools to pressing through every situation-ships and relationships is paramount. God has empowered a new breed of believers of faith to execute and exceed pass every barrier, by breaking through to new levels and greater territories in every area of their lives.

Luke 10:19, (KJV) says, Behold I give you the authority to trample on serpents and scorpions, and over all the power of the enemy, and nothing shall by any means hurt you.

The meaning of a GIANT is a mythical figure of superhuman size and strength. A person or thing of exceptional size and/or reputation. Something unusually so vast, humongous, and/or monstrous; Yet, GIANTS are simply the acronyms for the following: G=germs, I=initiate, A=annihilate, N=noise, T=turmoil, and S=SLAY. For every spiritual germ that attempts to assign itself to you: Initiate and annihilate the noise and the torment they say and SLAY THEM! "I Slay GIANTS," is an excellent vehicle for all to experience a complete healing and deliverance while helping others as you help yourself.

Endeavor, as we experience an epiphany of power, as we walk through this conquest from Victim Street to Victorious Boulevard.

Unlock your potentials within the truths and wisdom found in this book; For, it is revolutionary!

Jada R. Knowles
Pastor and Founder, Living Waters Apostolic Ministries
Atlanta, GA

YOU HOLD THE KEY

Table of Contents

Introduction

Inspiration

Let me begin by stating plainly that I serve the one true, mighty, living God, who gave his son as a living sacrifice so that I might live. It is through God's grace that I am saved. The Lord is present throughout this book. As I write, I hope these words create a sense of shared love, healing, restoration, and a true understanding of my testimony. I share because I can't navigate this journey alone. I share because I'm scared to be vulnerable. I share because if I can help even one person feel better, find some relief, or ease their anxiety, I'll feel like I've made a difference. One of my major "GIANTS" is fear, and I'll go into detail about my struggles with it later. I'm not trying to preach or force my beliefs on anyone. I'm simply sharing my story—my personal experience with the "GIANTS" in my life. This transparency is vulnerable for me, but it's how I overcame and continue to overcome the challenges in my life. If this isn't your cup of tea, that's perfectly fine. Everything isn't for everyone. I still love you, and I wouldn't want you to stop loving me just because we disagree. That's what starts wars.

A nervous energy fills me as I write this. It's the "what ifs" that are giving me butterflies. But anticipation is also building, giving me the courage to share my innermost thoughts. The desire to connect outweighs the idea of silently facing this battle alone. Everything has changed, even the way I think and process things. Sometimes, I feel scattered, ideas popping up constantly. I feel this need to get them out of my head and into words before I forget. Maybe that's just my cancer-related anxiety. I worry I'll miss a crucial detail and mess everything up. But I have to let that go and just flow. I want this to be easy for you to understand and to explain the different things I've experienced. I want you to understand the medical terms and discussions I include. Most of all, I want you to understand how I feel. Maybe there's something you'll identify with that will help you on your own journey.

My gurlz and I have a lovely relationship. My gurlz are my breasts. We've had a great relationship. It started pretty early in life. Around the age of 10ish, they just rolled up on the scene one day while purchasing Wonder Woman Underroos. While the other girls my age were in the girl section getting starter bras and cute matching underwear and bralettes, here I am in the woman's section of Sears getting my boobies pinched because, apparently, that's how you size them. The problem was then and always has been the assumption that because you need a bigger cup, you need a larger band. Uhhhhhh nawh. My grandmother is on another level with this bra thing because she didn't want any padding because she did not want my breasts to appear bigger than they already were. These were older women's bras, and I was only 10 years old, so definitely no colors. The bras that fit me were grown with lace or sheer inserts and my grandmother acted as if this thing was an application to work at a brothel. She ended up buying me this bra that looked like something out of the 1930s catalog that had both my gurlz looking like two bullet point props in a Madonna video. Needless to say, we found something practical by Playtex and thus began my journey with the gurlz.

They have always been here, full, proud and stable. I could always depend on them in times of sorrow, pain, and anxiousness.

There was comfort in their greatness. They fed my children, got me out of a couple of tickets, and were my shield against the world. First line of defense in a fight, they could take a punch. Sit up proud as I gave presentations and won awards and puff up proud when my babies shined. The gurlz went first. Now, is that a bosom for you or what? Or so I thought until I got sick.

The physical changes wrought by breast cancer, whether due to the disease itself or its treatment, often carry a significant emotional toll. These alterations to the body can impact a woman's sense of self, femininity, and overall well-being, adding another layer of complexity to an already challenging journey.

Hair loss, a common side effect of chemotherapy, can be particularly distressing. For many, hair is closely tied to identity and attractiveness, and its loss can trigger feelings of vulnerability and a diminished sense of control. Changes in weight, whether gain or loss, can also affect body image and self-confidence. Surgical procedures, such as mastectomies or lumpectomies, can lead to scarring and physical changes that may be difficult to accept. These changes can affect a woman's perception of her body and lead to feelings of self-consciousness or a sense of loss.

Beyond the visible changes, other physical effects, like fatigue, pain, and menopausal symptoms, can also take an emotional toll.

Constant fatigue can lead to frustration and a sense of disconnect from one's former life. Pain can be debilitating, impacting mood and the ability to engage in everyday activities. Menopausal symptoms, such as hot flashes and mood swings, can further disrupt emotional equilibrium.

The emotional impact of these physical changes can manifest in various ways. Some women may experience sadness, grief, or anger at the changes their bodies are undergoing. Others may struggle with feelings of anxiety, insecurity, or a loss of control. These emotional responses are normal and valid.

It's crucial for women experiencing these changes to have access to support systems, including mental health professionals, support groups, and open communication with their healthcare team. Therapy can provide a safe space to process emotions and develop coping strategies. Open communication with medical professionals ensures that physical symptoms are managed effectively, which can positively impact emotional well-being.

In conclusion, the physical changes associated with breast cancer can have profound emotional effects. It's important to acknowledge these emotional challenges and to seek support when needed. By addressing both the physical and emotional aspects of the breast cancer journey, women can work towards healing and reclaiming their sense of self.

Like A Daffodil

Like a daffodil, u fill
My happy thoughts w/bursts of laughter
Like a daffodil, u fill
My scary day's w/comfort, care & luv
Like a daffodil, each petal feels vibrant & strong
As u stand by my side thru disasters and harm,
Steadfast, unmovable thru all of my storms.
Ur joy and happiness always willing to share
When everyone leaves;
You are still standing there.
Like a daffodil u fill
My heart w/ gladness only
'cause u r who u r
Like a daffodil u fill my
Life w/hope, support &
luv
Like a daffodil, u r luved
Like a daffodil u r luved
Like a daffodil u r luved

My inspiration for this book is my sister Jocelyn. She is the next oldest female in our sibling group. You won't find a better person. Imagine, if you will, a person that you can always count on in times of trouble, no matter what it is. Imagine a person who is genuinely happy for your moments of shine and accomplishment. Imagine a person with whom you never have to question her intentions or wonder if her motives were ever malicious. A person who authentically recognizes and deciphers who you are truly and meets you right there when you interact. She is as sweet as pie when you need her to be but tough as nails when she has to be. You can rest assured her loyalty does not waiver, true to form… RIDAHHHHH: It is so beautiful how God has changed and evolved her. I repeat, she is such a sweet spirit. Always looking out for someone else, always blessing someone else, striving to endeavor to be a great mom, a wonderful wife, a lovable sister, and everything else that this woman of God does. She is my caregiver now since I need companionship. She has served as my cancer companion since the very beginning. She does whatever is in her power to lift you up. It is the small things that amaze me about her. Her sense of detail is immaculate. I mean down to taking out the trash after SHE helped me clean and organize all day. My sister can take an ordinary moment and show God's fingerprints all up and through the midst. I was ecstatic just the other day when she took us to get our nails done. My fingers match my toes, and I am, beside myself, cute, OK? OK. I could take up a few chapters of this book explaining to you guys all the wonderfulness this chic brings. It is my sister in the best way I can express her. She is just the BESTEST!

At about 5:00 AM Christmas Eve morning, my sister Jaye was on her way to work when she was carjacked at gunpoint. As I sat on the other end of that phone, my heart dropped. I felt a mix of emotions in a few seconds; I was scared, then worried, then surprised, then thankful, then mad again. Then I planned my revenge, how dare you? How dare you have the audacity to think your wants are important enough, bold enough to hold the decision or rather question my sister's life in your hands. Yo, who are these dudes? What do they look like? Did you get a license plate? They rolled up on her and tapped the window. I tried to picture how frightened and attacked she must have been, alone outside at the back of the house with my grandmother, 89 years old, and my 4-year-old nephew all asleep inside. Things could have gone wrong very fast. Thankfully, they didn't. I stayed on the phone with her until I heard the police and then I hung up. Joyce bubbled up so quickly. I wondered who I could reach out to and who I could ask for help. Joyce had some shady contacts that would have jumped at the opportunity to knuck and buck. You feel me? That part. But then I thought of God, and my perspective shifted.

Breast cancer has profoundly changed me. My thinking and processing are completely different, and its return and spread have brought even more change, but for the better. This whole experience triggered a strange memory, taking me back to a time after chemo when the fatigue, nausea, and listlessness were particularly intense. It was so hard to properly communicate these intangible symptoms; often, I just came across as sleepy. It's that feeling of helplessness, knowing you're not the person you used to be, and having to just watch things unfold. It's like watching your sister drown, and all you can do is feebly toss her a life preserver. So frustrating!

My sibling relationships are something most people can't quite grasp. There's no real discord between us. I don't know where I'd be without them. Now that we're all adults, we're inseparable. We all have spouses and children. Jaye is the sister who remembers every birthday and anniversary. Joy is always cheering you on, whether you're graduating, getting a promotion, receiving an award, stubbing your toe, or, back in the day, giving your boyfriend the boot. Her name says it all—she's pure joy. She's the "Stitch" of the family, a loving terror. And then there's my brother, Keith. You won't find a more loyal and loving man. He's like a modern-day male Mother Teresa. In short, my siblings are the best. Aaaaaaaaah!

I was always a fighter.

I have only lost one fight in my life, and that was to my best friend in 8th grade. We both became women in the same week and had some issues to resolve. We had been snapping at each other all that time, and I was fed up. We got into a scuffle over the class dictionary that day. A few overturned desks and bruises later, we sat in the principal's office, reflecting. She beat my tail. I guess she was more fed up than me. She and I were good friends and we both decided it was such a silly argument we made up before we even left the principal's office that day. I made a decision that day that I would not ever lose a fight again. I stuck to that vow, too. I can serve cancer this notice. **I'm not about to lose my reputation to no sickness.**

My mother and I were chatting the other day and she commented, "You know you always have been a fighter." I asked her about what she was talking about. My mother went on to state that during her pregnancy, I was the only child that she fasted and prayed for. She specifically asked for a girl I was born out of an answered prayer. A week after I was born, I developed a high fever. They rushed me to Children's Hospital in Philadelphia, where they ran all kinds of tests because they just could not figure out what was going on. The answers from all these tests that they ran finally led to a decision that they would need to do a spinal tap to assess my white blood cells. My mother stated that they had to call for backup because the one nurse who was trying to hold me down and administer the Spinal Tap said that she could not control me to hold me still. I was fighting too hard. They called in a second nurse who remarked that she had never seen a baby that could resist ...such a little thing. I had only been here for a week and was fighting them as if I had been here for months. It took two nurses to hold and a third to administer the Spinal Tap. In the end, it was diagnosed that I had a cold in my back and that antibiotics would do the trick to get rid of it and start me on the road back to recovery and health. All of this within one week of arriving here. It seems to me like I was fighting from the moment I got here. The very beginning.

My childhood memories are nice. I recently began talk therapy; I don't know how long it will last. This was one reason I delayed therapy until now. I was afraid of spoiling my childhood memories or finding some hidden secret that would shatter my world. It has not happened to date. It has been a good choice for my journey. Therapy would not have been on my top ten list until I was diagnosed with a condition that I absolutely have no control over. We came from a middle-class family, with the family home being in a neighborhood close to an Ivy League university, so the community was diverse. Our next-door neighbors, whom I grew up with, were my white friends who lived on the numbered streets. We roller-skated, played dollhouse, and did arts and crafts in their huge bedrooms. However, it would not be odd to find me jumping Double Dutch with my black girlfriends or doing steps or whatever on the name street side. I must be honest; I do not remember color or race being a factor in my play. I hung out and played with Sophie, Sarah, and Thomas just as much as I played with Dez, Julie, and Gina. It was not common for all of us to play together, though. I do, however, remember Sophie and Sarah both asking me to ask my mom if she would do their hair like Bo Derricks' hair on their daddy's magazine cover. I was the only diplomat traveling through my diverse groups of friends with ease of transition and for these two groups, fighting was not even a thing.

Nor was the notion that I could not do a thing or should not do a thing. Not one thing was I ever barred from thinking: I could be or have. I got exactly what I wanted. Now, the catch was and still to this day is, I still get what I want, but it's either not what everyone wants or how everyone else looks at it, or what everyone else likes. I don't care about others' opinions. In that little cocoon of Larchwood Street, although I was exposed to so many diverse things, outward perceptions begin to affect inward functions as you grow and fly away from the cocoon into the real world. Those days and influences did not seem that important, or were they?

My group of friends at my great-aunt's house deeper in West Philadelphia was a whole different world. University City in Philly ends around 51st, and then the real West Philly begins. The demographics change drastically within a single block, and by the time you hit 52nd Street...well, let's just say you're not in Kansas anymore, Toto. The zip code changes, and so does the whole vibe. This is the heart of urban Philly—you know, like Will Smith says, "In West Philadelphia, born and raised"—that part.

It was the '90s; hip-hop was everything. We rocked big gold hoops, name belts, and three-finger rings, trying to be the ultimate 'round-the-way girls. Life was good. EPMD was plotting their next move, and my girls and I were living out scenes from Brown Sugar and House Party simultaneously. And there I was, right in the thick of it. This was probably where I developed my warrior attitude and definitely where I got most of my fighting practice. My crew from 52nd Street—RBoogie, Tosh, Chelle, and Sherri—were all fighters, just like me.

My auntie's neighborhood would be considered the hood. Summertime would bring you open fire plugs with kids running around in cut-off jean shorts and T-shirts in the water. At the corner of a busy intersection, Mr. Softee set up blocking cars coming down the street and cutting across 53rd so others would have to form one lane to the left to pass. All the while, kids of all ages and the adults dragged out of the house screaming, "iceee creeeamm…" almost out of breath packed the street even more. Grandmothers sat out on the front porch with the church fans, fanning feverishly to stay cool. They didn't even realize that the action of fanning themselves made them hotter than if they just sat still and let the cool breeze flow. Somebody's stereo, either out the house window or beatbox posted on the stoop, would be blasting EPMD, Summertime by the Fresh Prince, or my favorite, "Push It!" by Salt n Pepa. Fresh smells of Chinese food from the store across the street or fried chicken from the neighbors wafted across your nose. We could go to any of those wonderful open doors and be invited in to indulge in all the good-smelling delicacies of summer. Smelled good, smelled real good…smelled like home to me.

The neighborhood drug dealers and young guys hanging on the corner of 53rd and Chancellor were a summer staple. You'd hear them shooting dice, riding bikes, and doing wheelies. They were always catcalling girls walking by from the Primp and Pamper salon around the corner. Everyone knew what they were up to, but like everything else, they were just part of the landscape. Back then, the leader of the young guys was Pootie Dawg. I never knew his real name (what we called a person's "government" name, especially if you knew their middle name—it's what my mother used when we were in trouble).

Pootie Dawg had a younger brother whose name I never knew, and they ran with a group of four or five guys all about the same age. We called them the Peach Street boys. While Pootie and his crew held down their territory in their own ways, his little brother's crew was more into mischief and mayhem—like that insurance commercial—and were just a general pain in the butt.

Now, I will not have you all thinking that I was just running the streets of West Philly wilding out. That was not the case at all. There were rules and codes of conduct on those streets. Some things you just did not do, and boys fighting girls was a no-go. At my aunt's house, when we hung out, she held a pretty strict hold on my goings and comings. I was usually relegated to the porch, and that started from the time I got my period until I turned eighteen and stopped spending time there. Her thought process was the minute I turned into a woman, I could get pregnant, and she was going to make sure it was not on her watch. No biggie for me, thought. That was not even my twist. The good thing about me being a fighter was that I was more interested in fighting the boys than I was in f******g them. This is how I ended up in that summer's free fall fight.

One day, on my way home from choir practice, I came upon a disturbance. In the middle of the street was my girlfriend Tosh, arguing with one of the Peach Street boys. He was all up in her mug, and she had to push him to make him back up off of her. When her hands touched his chest to get him out of her face, two of the other boys jumped in her face as well, and one walked up behind her so she could not step back. Looked to me like the biggest problem was she was a girl, and there were 4 of them up in her face. My girlfriend had her hands up, ready to fight. She had on a long jean skirt that she had pulled up to her waist. It was about to go down. I immediately ran towards the commotion and positioned myself between her and Pootie Dawg's brother. I pushed him out of her face, and he stumbled backward. At that same moment, the boy standing behind Tosh shoved her. The next thing I knew, I was squaring up, and so was she. The two boys that were in her face before ran up on the sidewalk while we commenced whipping ass in the streets. You could hear the other boys on the sideline trying to cheer their counterparts on, but it was to no avail. Pootie Dawg came off the corner to intervene when everything screamed to a halt with a gun shot in the air. Here my great uncle had walked down to the corner to see what all the commotion was because I was not on the porch. When he saw me fighting, he took his rusty pistol, which, thank God, had not jammed or backfired and shot up in the air. He yelled at the Peach Street boys to get off his niece and told them the next shot would be in their ass. Now I am nervous as hell because I beat up the big wig's little brother, and I did not really think about whether the older boys like Pootie were packing. Jesus help! My girlfriend and I were ushered back down the street to the porch, and our parents were called. Funny thing, I would get in trouble every time I fought with my mom. My uncle was just beside himself because at 80 something, it was not ladylike for women to fight … definitely not boys and definitely not winning. Oh God, I was just the worst. Shoot, if I was not preggers, I thought I was on top of the world. Better I beat on them than have their babies, I thought. The day the radiologist brought me in to confirm that I indeed had breast cancer, I felt the same way. I felt like there was this big bully, cancer, and its cronies who jumped my left bosom, traumatized it, violated me personally, and I was getting ready to fight.

My spiritual foundation also began at my auntie's house. It's funny how the same place I learned to fight was also where I learned about God. My Aunt Clora was a devout churchgoer. Every Sunday, we were getting up early for Sunday school and service at Zion Hill on 53rd and Spruce. Zion Hill was a typical Baptist church, complete with ushers in white, deacon and deaconess boards, a pastor's auxiliary, a Mother's board, a mass choir, men's choir, children's choir—the whole nine yards. Back then, Aunt Clora was our connection to God. My mom wasn't in church at the time, so we didn't have that typical church family dynamic.

This is important: whenever there was an issue where an adult felt I needed discipline, they couldn't go to my mother. They had to go to my eighty-something-year-old great-great-grandmother's sister—my aunt Clora. Talk about an age gap! So, I always had to defend myself. If you asked anyone at the church, they'd say I was sweet and wonderful, but I also had an attitude and a mouth on me.

First of all, I've never tolerated being talked to disrespectfully. It's a trigger for me, and it doesn't matter who it's coming from. It stops with me, believe that. One deacon at the church always had something to criticize or some silly excuse to scold me. One day, while I was out on one of my forbidden (but frequent) adventures on 52nd Street, I ran into this same deacon coming out of the Ponytail Bar—the neighborhood strip club! Why was he there?! In my sweetest voice, I chirped, "Heeeeyyyyyy, Deacon So-and-So!" I made sure he knew I saw him and where he was coming from.

The very next Sunday, he confronted me. "Does your mother know you wear so much makeup?" (I only wore eyeliner and lip gloss, then. I guess it was the eyeliner that bothered him.) He kept saying I looked like a grown woman. I told him I wasn't and to take it up with my auntie. I added that if it was such a problem, I was sure Deaconess So-and-So would love to know he was harassing me. I'd be happy to tell her about his comments and the fact that he was at the strip club on Saturday night, drinking and doing who knows what else, and then supposedly praising God and bothering me at church the next day.

He just stuttered, wide-eyed, and accused me of sassing him, asking who I thought I was. I asked him the same thing since he wasn't my daddy. In my innocence, I told him I didn't even know who my father was, but I knew it wasn't him. After that, he never bothered me again. Yes, leave me alone, sir. You don't scare me. Deacon So-and-So turned out to be just one of the first "GIANTS" I had to slay. I didn't realize it then, but it was a crucial lesson.

A father to the fatherless.

This topic deserves its own chapter. I didn't realize this "GIANT" – the absence of a father – had so many facets until I got sick. Growing up without a dad, I'd see ads with happy families—mom, dad, kids—having dinner or playing games, and I longed for that. It never really happened. That missing piece in my upbringing became even more pronounced when I thought I was dying. I felt rejected and hurt. It felt like one more thing that made me different. But I wasn't looking at it the right way. I was focused on what I didn't have rather than what I did. Cancer makes you take stock of your life. You examine all your relationships and weigh them against one question: "If I die tomorrow, will this even matter?" Changing my focus got me through it. When I look back, I realize how many blessings I have.

Growing up without a father can leave a lasting impact that extends into adulthood, shaping various aspects of an individual's life. While every experience is unique, some common themes emerge in the narratives of those raised in father-absent homes. These effects can range from emotional challenges to relationship dynamics and self-perception.

One significant area often affected is emotional well-being. The absence of a father figure can leave a void, leading to feelings of abandonment, insecurity, and a struggle with self-worth. Adults who grew up without fathers may experience difficulties with emotional regulation, trust, and intimacy. They might struggle to express emotions healthily or have a heightened sensitivity to rejection. The lack of a consistent male role model can also impact their understanding of masculinity and their own identity as men or women.

Relationships, particularly romantic ones, can be complex for adults who have experienced a father's absence. They may have difficulty forming secure attachments, fearing abandonment, or struggling with vulnerability. For some, the absence of a father can lead to seeking validation or approval from partners, sometimes repeating unhealthy relationship patterns. Others might avoid intimacy altogether, fearing the pain of potential loss. These challenges can stem from a lack of understanding of healthy relationship dynamics, often influenced by the absence of a parental example.

Self-esteem and self-perception can also be affected. Growing up without a father can lead to feelings of inadequacy or a sense that something is missing. Adults might struggle with confidence, particularly in situations that require assertiveness or leadership. They may also experience a greater need for external validation, seeking approval from others to compensate for the lack of a father's affirmation.

It's important to acknowledge that resilience and strength can also emerge from these experiences. Many individuals raised without fathers develop strong self-reliance, independence, and empathy. They may cultivate close relationships with other family members or mentors who provide support and guidance. The challenges they face can fuel a drive to succeed and create a better life for themselves.

In conclusion, the effects of growing up without a father can be varied and complex. While challenges related to emotional well-being, relationships, and self-perception are common, it's crucial to recognize the individual nature of these experiences. Many adults who grew up without fathers find ways to thrive, build strong support systems, and create fulfilling lives. Understanding the potential impact of a father's absence can foster greater empathy and support for those navigating these unique life journeys. (Father absence and trajectories of offspring mental health across adolescence and young adulthood: Findings from a UK-birth cohortpmc.ncbi.nlm.nih.gov, How our Family Relationships Impacts Us: The Father Wound - Alive Counselling alivecounselling.com, The relationship between father absence and hostility among Chinese depressed youths: A serial mediation model and the role of self-esteem and frustration tolerance - PubMed Centralpmc.ncbi.nlm.nih.gov)

How is God a father to the fatherless? When I got diagnosed I was missing a "Dad" especially when they started to ask questions about my paternal side. I knew nothing. This complex question has been pondered by theologians and individuals for centuries. Here are some perspectives to consider:

1. God as the ultimate source of love and care:

Many believe that God fills the void left by an absent or imperfect father figure. He offers unconditional love, support, and guidance to those who feel lost or abandoned. This idea is rooted in the concept of God as a loving and compassionate parent who cares deeply for all his children.

2. God as the provider and protector:

In many cultures, fathers are seen as the primary providers and protectors of their families. Some believe that God takes on this role for the fatherless, ensuring their needs are met and they are kept safe. This can manifest in various ways, such as providing for their material needs, guiding them towards positive relationships, or protecting them from harm.

3. God as the source of identity and belonging:

For those who have experienced the pain of losing a father or never having one, it can be difficult to establish a sense of identity and belonging. Some believe that God offers a new identity to the fatherless, one rooted in his love and acceptance. This can provide a sense of purpose and belonging that transcends earthly relationships.

4. The role of community and support:

While God's love and care are central to the concept of fatherhood for the fatherless, many also emphasize the importance of community and support from others. This can include mentors, role models, or other caring adults who can provide guidance and support.

It's important to note that these are just some of the ways in which God is seen as a father to the fatherless. Ultimately, the meaning and interpretation of this concept will vary depending on individual beliefs and experiences.

The concept of God as a father can be comforting and empowering for those who have experienced loss or abandonment. It can also be a source of hope and resilience, reminding them that they are not alone and are loved unconditionally. It's important to acknowledge that the pain of losing a father or never having one is real and valid. Ultimately, the question of how God is a father to the fatherless is a personal one. It's something that each individual must explore and answer for themselves.

I want to pause here and honor my mother, grandmother, and great-grandmother. The amazingly strong, powerful women of the Trotman family. A testament to just how strong and tenacious they were and are in the absence of proper male representation and support.

My family was led by these strong women: my great-great-grandmother Gigi, my glamorous grandmother GBoog, and my mom, who, though married, was practically a single mother and taught me what it means to be a strong Black woman. But I haven't mentioned any men. I stated I grew up without a dad; to this day I don't know who he is. I had two great uncles, but they were much older. This is a difficult subject for me, especially to talk about publicly. I don't know why my father is absent. Growing up, I heard negative things about him from older relatives who didn't like him or perhaps wanted to hurt me. I learned he was in the army and from West Philly. I know I have siblings close to my age, even sharing birthdays. But I still have so many unanswered questions and "what ifs." Growing up with that missing piece in my foundation made everything feel unsteady. And when difficult situations arose, like my cancer diagnosis, it felt like everything was crumbling. I wondered, "What if the women on his side have a history of this disease?" All those questions were answered when I took the BRCA test. It showed no genetic mutations for breast cancer or other cancers from either side of my family. I can't pass this on to my children. Hallelujah!

BRCA testing is a process that analyzes DNA to identify changes, or mutations, in the BRCA1 and BRCA2 genes. These genes play a crucial role in DNA repair, and mutations can increase the risk of developing certain cancers, most notably breast and ovarian cancer. Understanding BRCA testing involves considering who might benefit, what the process entails, and what the implications of the results can be.

Individuals with a family history of breast, ovarian, or other related cancers, particularly at a young age, are often considered candidates for BRCA testing. Other risk factors, such as Ashkenazi Jewish heritage or a personal history of certain cancers, may also prompt a recommendation for testing. A genetic counselor can help assess an individual's risk and determine if testing is appropriate.

The BRCA test itself typically involves a blood or saliva sample. The collected cells are then analyzed in a lab to look for specific mutations in the BRCA1 and BRCA2 genes. The process can take several weeks to receive results.

The results of BRCA testing can be complex. A positive result indicates a mutation is present, significantly increasing the risk of developing certain cancers. However, it's important to remember that a positive result doesn't guarantee a cancer diagnosis. It provides information that can be used to make informed decisions about risk reduction strategies, such as increased surveillance, medication, or preventative surgery. A negative result, while reassuring, doesn't eliminate the risk of cancer, especially if there's a strong family history. Sometimes, the test results are inconclusive, meaning a change was found in the gene, but it's unclear if it increases cancer risk. This uncertainty can be challenging to navigate.

Ultimately, BRCA testing is a personal decision. It's essential to discuss the potential benefits and risks with a doctor or genetic counselor to make an informed choice. Understanding the implications of the results, both positive and negative, is critical for anyone considering this type of genetic test. (BRCA Gene Changes: Cancer Risk and Genetic Testing Fact Sheet – NCI www.cancer.gov, Understanding BRCA Gene Testing for Breast and Ovarian Cancer Risk |Charlotte Radiology www.charlotteradiology.com, Genetic Testing for Hereditary Breast and Ovarian Cancer - CDCwww.cdc.gov)

John L. Trotman was my “Big Daddy " who lived right down there in Dothan, Alabama. I loved driving down there with GiGi in the summer with my siblings, mom, and grandma. The thing is, my GiGi was not my Big Mama. Big Mama lived with Big Daddy in Dothan. In those times, families did not really get into the intricacies of divorce and remarriage. Now that I think of it, they did not get into blended families either because all my life I thought my grandmother was an only child, but I know Big Daddy and Big Mamma had children, a boy. I think Gigi was an angel assigned to us here on Earth.

You cannot tell me anything, but She was the oldest of three children by her mother. Ethel Mae Trotman was her name. Then there was my aunt Clora and my uncle Willie Anderson, whom we called "Uncle Buddy Boy.

My great-grandmother had a beautiful, fair, smooth complexion. Long, smooth, shiny black hair thanks to the Cherokee Indian blood in her veins, the Clairol box in the bathroom trash basket, and the Vigorol pressing oil in the drawer next to the stove and pressing comb. Something happened to her left leg, and it no longer bent at the knee. She had a determined walk and did not use any assistive device such as a cane or walker. She walked upright, proud and stunning, better than any fashion model you would see. She worked in Wanamaker's downtown within the sporty woman section. This was the area for the hip upcoming fashions, the runway for the women's department. One thing you can be assured of is that my Gigi was always sharp, Period!! She was an industrious woman who bought her house in an upscale neighborhood that originally was mostly white. Her disability never was a disability for her. Even with the inability to move her leg she still walked with a determined purpose, with a steady stroll, and with a dignified air. Nothing about that injured or immobilized leg immobilized her or hindered her from doing anything that she set her mind to doing. My first lessons in determination are from Gigi because she was an "in spite of" type of lady. I wanted to be just like her, loving, kind, and just. Excessively beautiful, tall, and elegant without a trace of "Rasheeka" in her. Her catwalk was better than Naomi Campbell's if you asked me, and her stature was taller than Rue Paul's. She was elegance personified right in front of this little Black girl's eyes. If racism was a thing in the seventies…I had no clue. She could hang out with the best of them.

Dressed to the nine for cocktail parties, events, and venues with the elite with outfits from Saks and Wanamaker's, appliances, and dinnerware from Sears RoebuckPepsi and Mountain Dew on tap, and I had NO CLUE what the hell layaway was. Whatever we wanted, we, being me, my momma, and grandmother, got right then and there. That is how life was when GiGi was living. She taught me how to handle disability and to hold my head high in spite of physical difficulties.

BREAST CANCER

The Diagnosis

A cancer diagnosis, especially the "Big C," is a huge challenge, and it comes with a lot of stress. My first mammogram in 2021 immediately showed something abnormal in both breasts. In fact, the technician told me when I returned for the biopsy that she could feel the tumor in my left breast while positioning me. Waiting for test results is incredibly difficult, so be prepared for that. If you're a worrier like me, I strongly suggest finding a good therapist as soon as you're diagnosed. I know mental health is often stigmatized, especially in my community, which I don't understand. When your body is sick, you seek professional help. Why not for your mind? You see an oncologist for your cancer; why is there a problem seeing a therapist or psychiatrist if needed? You take medicine for your body; why not for your mind? Now is not the time to think you can handle everything alone. If you find yourself in this situation, tell your oncologist so they can refer you to someone. Cancer is traumatic, with all the appointments, scans, and tests.

My experience might not be typical. I had a biopsy scheduled for both breasts. They numbed the area and took a sample using a needle with a tiny blade that snapped out and cut a small piece of the tumor. It sounded like a staple gun, but I didn't feel anything. When they tried to sample the tumor in my right breast, it collapsed—it wasn't a tumor at all, but a fluid-filled cyst. Let me emphasize the importance of breast screenings. I know younger people don't hear this often, but most screenings are free, and they will screen you if you ask. Screenings also teach you how to do self-exams, which is great.

The very next day, I met with the radiologist. She carefully reviewed the scan with me, explaining her concerns. She pointed out the tumor, which looked enormous to me—an almost 8cm barbell-shaped lump with two bulges and a middle section. The tumor the technician had felt was obvious now, as if it had always been there. The exam room suddenly felt small with all the people there—the radiologist, technicians, and my sister—explaining what they'd found. Looking back, it reminds me of a fight. There was no way I was taking this lying down. I was going to fight.

I started by building a support team. I designated one person to accompany me to chemotherapy, appointments, and tests and to manage my medications. Another person was there for emotional support to keep my spirits up. A third person managed my calendar so I wouldn't miss any appointments or tests.

Now, you might not have three separate people. You might have one amazing person, like my sister, who handles everything. The point is that you need support during this time. It's best to get your support system in place early and make sure everyone understands their roles and responsibilities. If someone can't or doesn't fulfill their duties, they need to be replaced, just like in a job. You're the boss here.

Chemotherapy

The day I started chemotherapy, I had a port installed. It was a small device that was used primarily to administer chemotherapy treatments and to draw blood without sticking me a bunch of times. It was placed under my skin over my right breast (it goes on the unaffected side) in about an hour in outpatient surgery. It is done under local anesthesia, and you can ask for something to calm your nerves from your oncologist the day before. The port connected to a central line, also known as a PICC line or a porta Cath, and was threaded through a large vein in my neck.

Chemo can be incredibly challenging. It's definitely one of the "GIANTS" you might face with cancer. Not everyone with breast cancer undergoes chemotherapy, but it's a common treatment. I mentioned a drug regimen called AC+T. This is shorthand for a combination of three drugs nicknamed "the red devil" because they look like bright red Kool-Aid on a hot day. But trust me, they're nowhere near as refreshing. Healthcentral.com explains that AC+T includes doxorubicin (Adriamycin), cyclophosphamide (Cytoxan), and a taxane drug (Taxol or Taxotere).

A (Adriamycin) stops cells from making DNA, which kills them, especially cancer cells that divide fast.

C (Cyclophosphamide) stops cancer cells from multiplying.

T (Taxol or Taxotere) slows or stops cell division and prevents cells from making the proteins they need to grow[1]. (What Is TC (Taxotere and Cytoxan) Chemotherapy for Breast Cancer?

https://www.healthcentral.com/article/chemo-regimen-faqs-ac-taxoltaxotere-chemotherapy-act-tac)

Nausea/Vomiting	Sour Patch Kids; Lemon Mike & Ike's; SweetTarts: take meds proactively; stay hydrated
Hair Loss/ Thinning	Special Hair Oil mix; Warm, Soft Cap/ head wraps for chills even in the house
Fatigue/Weakness	Pace yourself; say NO if you are not up to it; multivitamins (if allowed); supplements (if allowed); iron infusions (if prescribed); walk in place (build to 30 mins a day)
Cognitive Injury Impairment	CIT (cognitive impairment therapy); Luminosity; AARP Brain Games; puzzles
Acute Kidney Injury	Stay Hydrated; Consult/Monitor w/nephrologist

Dry Skin	Dove products; Ooyoni Soap & Spray; Castor Oil: Special Skin Oil for Face, Neck, & Breast (all self-made)
Diarrhea/Loose Stools	Imodium; Pedialyte/Gatorade
Panic Attacks	Any song by WHAM! Or Micheal Jackson ;Prayer; Meditation; Talk Therapy; Prescribed Medication; Square Breathing;
Joint Pain	Turmeric supplements
Hot Flashes	Personal mini fans; mineral water spritz
Dehydration	64 to 80 oz daily fluid intake
Constipation	Increase fluid intake; Colace stool softener Dr supervised
Weird taste	Plastic Utensils; Avoid spicy foods; Avoid mushy foods (al-dente); Don't add salt; Avoid red and blue food coloring
Retinal hemorrhage	Maintain proper BP
Dark Nail Beds	Lemon juice soaks: gel Mani-Pedi (* if allowed)

My chemo drugs currently are Carboplatin and Gemcitabine. I call them the "G" and the "C". They make a combo called

GemCarbo. Some of my side effects have stayed the same. Some have increased. There are things that I experience now that I did not have to contend with my first go round. Effects are as follows with my personal tricks for comfort:

Support - A breast cancer diagnosis can be a life-altering event, bringing about a range of emotions such as fear, anxiety, sadness, and uncertainty. In such challenging times, emotional support plays a crucial role in helping patients cope with the physical and psychological impact of the disease.

Emotional support can come from various sources, including family, friends, support groups, healthcare professionals, and even online communities. These support systems provide a safe space for patients to express their feelings, share their experiences, and receive encouragement and understanding.

Family and friends can offer practical assistance, such as accompanying patients to appointments or helping with household chores. They can also provide emotional comfort by listening, offering words of affirmation, and simply being present.

Support groups, whether in-person or online, connect breast cancer patients with others who understand their journey. Sharing experiences and coping strategies with peers can reduce feelings of isolation and empower patients to take an active role in their care.

Healthcare professionals, including doctors, nurses, and therapists, provide not only medical expertise but also emotional guidance. They can address patients' concerns, offer reassurance, and help them navigate the complex healthcare system.

In addition to these traditional forms of support, online communities and social media platforms have emerged as valuable resources for breast cancer patients. These platforms offer a sense of connection and allow patients to share information, ask questions, and find support from others around the world.

The benefits of emotional support for breast cancer patients are well-documented. Studies have shown that strong social support can improve quality of life, reduce stress and anxiety, and even enhance treatment outcomes. By fostering a sense of belonging, empowerment, and hope, emotional support can help patients navigate the challenges of breast cancer and maintain a positive outlook.

In conclusion, emotional support is essential for breast cancer patients. Whether it comes from family, friends, support groups, healthcare professionals, or online communities, emotional support can make a significant difference in a patient's journey, helping them cope with the emotional and physical challenges of the disease and improve their overall well-being.

Nausea/Vomiting - My nausea and subsequent vomiting would hit me just like morning sickness when I was pregnant with my children. The feeling starts as a rumbling in your stomach. Next up is a hot flash, and you start sweating a little. The next symptom is slight Vertigo, where I would feel lightheaded, so I would usually need to sit down. I would hold my head in between my knees. My mouth would suddenly fill up with warm, salty saliva. I knew I had to spit it out, or I would vomit for sure. I would use a small trash bin with scented plastic bags in it. I would get the ones that smell like pine because that aroma helps me with the nausea. I would just lean over the bin and let the fluid run out of my mouth without force. I would follow this with some sour candy like Sour Patch Kids or Lemon Mike and Ike's. Extremely sour Warheads work wonders and stave off nausea enough for me to take one of my Compazine or Zofran pills. Sometimes, this technique would not work. I would just be too far gone. One of the transfusion nurses taught me a neat trick and told me that instead of taking my anti-nausea medicine at the start of an episode, to take it regularly every six hours during the day for the Compazine and then Zofran at night because it lasts 8 hours to hold me until morning. This tip has helped me immensely, and I now only get occasional bouts of nausea, usually in the mornings, and a breakthrough maybe later in the day here and there, as opposed to frequent episodes, two or three times a day.

Prayer/ Meditation - Prayer and meditation, often used as complementary practices, can offer significant emotional and spiritual support to individuals navigating the challenges of breast cancer. While not a replacement for medical treatment, these practices can positively influence well-being and coping mechanisms during a difficult time.

Prayer, for many, provides a direct line of communication with a higher power, offering solace, hope, and a sense of connection. It can be a source of comfort in the face of fear and uncertainty, allowing individuals to express their anxieties, seek guidance, and find strength in their faith. The act of prayer can also foster a sense of control and agency, empowering patients to actively participate in their healing journey. Furthermore, communal prayer, whether in a religious setting or with loved ones, can create a strong support network and a shared sense of purpose.

Meditation, on the other hand, focuses on quieting the mind and cultivating a state of inner peace. Through mindfulness and focused breathing techniques, meditation can help reduce stress, anxiety, and depression, which are common emotional side effects of a cancer diagnosis and treatment. Regular meditation practice can also improve sleep quality, boost the immune system, and enhance overall well-being. By promoting relaxation and self-awareness, meditation can empower patients to manage their symptoms and cope more effectively with the challenges of their illness.

It's important to note that the benefits of prayer and meditation are often intertwined. For many, prayer is a form of meditation, a focused and intentional connection with the divine. Both practices can foster a sense of hope, resilience, and connection to something larger than oneself. They can also provide a sense of meaning and purpose during a time when life can feel overwhelming and uncertain.

While research on the direct impact of prayer and meditation on cancer outcomes is ongoing, studies have shown that these practices can significantly improve quality of life, reduce stress hormones, and enhance emotional well-being in cancer patients. Ultimately, the decision to incorporate prayer and meditation into a cancer care plan is a personal one. However, those who find comfort and strength in these practices can be valuable tools for navigating the emotional and spiritual challenges of breast cancer.(Religion and Spirituality: their Role in the Psychosocial Adjustment to Breast Cancer and Subsequent Symptom Management of Adjuvant Endocrine Therapypmc.ncbi.nlm.nih.gov, The Science of Prayer

(www.psychologicalscience.org, The effects of prayer on attention resource availability and attention bias - PMC pmc.ncbi.nlm.nih.gov)

Hair Loss/ Thinning - On the second dose of my chemo treatment, when I was on ACT, I lost my hair. I called myself getting ahead of the challenge by shaving all my hair really short and dying it hot pink. Still came out to the root, and I was bald through the A and C cycles until I hit just the Taxol. It took me about six months to grow back a fine grade of curly hair after my first cycle of chemo. This time around with the GemCarbo regimen, my hair is a fine, curly, short afro, which I'm planning to be paprika red by the time this book is published. I made a special hair growth oil that I massage into my scalp in the morning and in the evenings before bed. I will put the link to all the items I mentioned on the reference page.

Fatigue/Weakness - I would like to emphasize the need to advocate for yourself, your needs, and your wants. Fighting cancer of any type and going through treatments like chemotherapy, radiation, or immunotherapy is draining. They require a lot of energy. You are the best judge of your own energy levels. You need to convince people that you need to rest. You need to make it happen! Sometimes, on this journey, you won't have enough energy to care about what anyone else wants or expects from you. You know how much rest helps you recover. It's not the same as when you were healthy. Find something that calms you and helps you sleep. My final advice on fatigue and weakness is to seek help. You are just not going to be able to do the things that you are used to doing, not only for others but for yourself. Something simple as putting on socks or getting washed up in the morning can be a daunting task as you're contending with cancer. Don't be afraid or ashamed to ask for help.

Cognitive Damage Effects - I used to think chemo brain was not real, just like pregnancy brain. I attributed it to me being careless or distracted. I did not even realize there was an issue until I resumed work. When I began chemotherapy, I worked partly from home in a customer service role. There were no time restraints, more so a certain volume that you had to hit weekly. At that time, I didn't feel any effects, but I returned to work full time in a similar environment, with the same amount and kind of service calls. There, I saw the difference! I was much slower than my colleagues and my numbers showed it. My attention would wander. I would lose track of why I got up or what I planned to do. It would take me a while to sort out my thoughts. When I wanted to say something, I would forget a word and couldn't recall it for anything. As you can imagine, all of this was highly frustrating. When I told my oncologist about the new things that I was experiencing, it was identified as a cognitive brain injury. CRCI, to be more exact, Cancer Related to Cognitive Impairment.

Chemo Brain (Cancer-Related Cognitive Impairment) causes trouble with thinking and memory during treatment. My cancer treatment involved chemotherapy, radiation therapy, surgery, and other drugs. Since then, I have had and still struggle with memory loss, concentration problems, multitasking issues, and a general sense of fogginess. Chemo brain also makes me prone to panic attacks and adds to anxiety. Some ways to cope with chemo brain are cognitive rehabilitation, lifestyle changes, and help from specialists.(cancerresearchuk.org)

Chemotherapy may cause kidney damage in some cases. This is a condition called nephrotoxicity. It happens because the kidneys' role is to process and clear out chemotherapy drugs from the body, and this can produce substances that hurt kidney cells. Here are some important points to consider: Prevention: To help prevent serious kidney damage, doctors may offer more fluid in infusions during chemotherapy treatments and prescribe protective medications.(https://www.healthline.com/health/kidney-health/how-to-protect-your-kidneys-during-chemotherapy)

Dry Skin - Dry skin is a frequent side effect of cancer treatments like chemotherapy and radiation. Several factors contribute to this dryness. Here are some tips for managing it:

- Regular Skin Checks: Frequently examine your skin for any changes like roughness, redness, flakiness, swelling, itching, or cracking.
- Hydration: Drink plenty of water each day to stay hydrated.
- Avoid Alcohol-Based Products: Steer clear of skincare products containing alcohol, as these can further dry out the skin.
- Short, Warm Showers: Limit shower time and use lukewarm water. Hot showers can strip your skin of its natural oils. Avoid harsh exfoliants while bathing. Gently pat your skin dry afterward.

- Moisturize: Apply moisturizer immediately after showering to lock in moisture.

- Skin Protection: Avoid hot water and dry heat. If you shave, use an electric razor.

- Consult Your Healthcare Provider: If your skin becomes very rough, red, or painful, seek medical advice. Also, notify your healthcare team if you notice any signs of infection or bleeding. (verywellhealth.com)

Diarrhea/Loose Stools - Fortunately enough, I have not had to deal with a lot of episodes of diarrhea or loose stools. I have Imodium prescribed for when these situations do occur, and I take it as instructed by my oncologist, which is 2 pills at the first loose stool and one thereafter until it stops. I would suggest you consult with your physician before taking any medication over the counter or otherwise.

Panic Attacks - I experienced one panic attack before I was diagnosed with cancer. It was a day that I had gotten into a confrontation with my manager over something I thought was unfair. I was reprimanded, and the decision was made to put a note in my file that I had no control over. Something about not being heard in my defense that day caused me to just snap, for lack of a better word. On the drive home that day, I had to pull over to the side of the road and gather myself. My breathing and heart rate were way up. It seemed as if I were going to pass out from lack of oxygen. I was crying uncontrollably, and it didn't seem like it was ever going to stop. That day, I distinctly remember DJ Touch Tone on the radio playing “I’ll Take Ya Man” by Salt 'n Pepa. They say music soothes the savage beast. There is something about belting out your favorite song from your soul that frees you in a tense moment, and I am no different.

My present-day panic attacks generate sheer fear. The night of the biopsy, Philly had a bad storm that knocked the power out for over an hour. Five minutes into the event, I was on the verge of an attack. I felt this one coming, though. There it was, the increased short breaths. Then I broke into a bad sweat. It seemed, for some reason, that the dark was enveloping me, trying to swallow me whole. That night, I used the flashlight from my phone as a beacon of light in the darkness. I played pink noise, and it helped calm my nerves. I also set up a few candles whose soft glow helped alleviate a portion of the angst from the ordeal. At least there were no more shadow monsters trying to swallow me whole. I had no idea PTSD could develop from a battle with cancer. It is a traumatic experience. You visit and revisit scary experiences all the time. The best thing about cancer is that it puts you face to face with any underlying issues affecting your health. Your mental state is one of those issues. It matters. Your mind can heal your body. What’s in your heart dictates what you think about. You need that right now. I offer 3 words to **seek… professional… help**.

Music Therapy - Music therapy is often overlooked, which is a shame. I love how music can shift my mood, no matter what's going on. It's like my life could have a soundtrack—certain songs just perfectly capture moments and thoughts. I consider my musical abilities, the harmonies I can hear, a real gift. I can pick out the patterns, notes, keys, and instruments individually, even the different vocal ranges. I can tell if something's even slightly off in the harmony. Music is my comfort, my balm.

Music is universal. A song that sounds good to me will resonate with someone anywhere, regardless of language. I could be in Japan listening to an orchestra and feel it just as deeply as if I were in my bedroom. It transcends time, space, arguments, war, death, pain, difficulties, and any differences between us. It's how I personally worship. Music helps me praise God, who, like music, transcends all situations, even something like a cancer diagnosis. I'll sing happy songs until I actually feel happy. Sad songs have helped me through so much. Come on, ladies, how many of us have sat still through "Walk It Out"? If that song came on right now, we'd all be up dancing! Or how about "Go ahead now, go walk out the door.."? Music really does soothe the soul.

Pain – This is another area where I encourage you to speak up and make sure your voice is heard. That is when it comes to pain. NOBODY else's interpretation of what you are feeling matters. Your comfort is of the utmost importance. Usually, pain is rated on a 0 to 10 scale, with 10 being the worst ever. Be honest about your number; don't feel as if you need to dummy down your number for any reason. If it's a 9, then dang it, it's a 9. At no point do I want you to feel like you have to suffer through ANY amount of discomfort. In any form, PAIN should be discussed with your doctors, and if it's a continual pain or goes above your pain threshold number, ask to be referred to the pain team.

Managing pain in breast cancer patients is a complex but crucial aspect of care. Pain can arise from the cancer itself, its treatment, or related conditions, significantly impacting quality of life. A multifaceted approach tailored to the individual is essential for effective pain management.

One of the first steps is a thorough assessment of the pain. This involves understanding the location, intensity, nature (e.g., sharp, aching, burning), and duration of the pain, as well as what factors trigger or alleviate it. Patients should openly communicate with their healthcare team about their pain experience, as this information is vital for developing a personalized pain management plan.

Pain management strategies for breast cancer patients can be broadly categorized into pharmacological and non-pharmacological approaches. Pharmacological interventions often involve pain medications, which may include over-the-counter pain relievers like acetaminophen or ibuprofen for mild pain or stronger opioids for more severe pain. The choice of medication and dosage will depend on the type and intensity of pain, as well as the patient's overall health and other medications they may be taking. It's crucial that pain medication is taken as prescribed and that any side effects are reported to the healthcare team.

Non-pharmacological approaches play a vital role in pain management and can often be used in conjunction with medication. These methods may include physical therapy to improve mobility and reduce pain, massage therapy to relax muscles and ease tension, and acupuncture, which may help to reduce certain types of pain.

Mind-body techniques, such as meditation, deep breathing exercises, and guided imagery, can also be helpful in managing pain by reducing stress and promoting relaxation. These techniques can empower patients to actively participate in their pain management.

Complementary therapies, such as aromatherapy, can also be explored. While research on the effectiveness of these therapies for cancer pain is ongoing, some patients find them helpful in reducing discomfort and promoting relaxation. It is important to discuss any complementary therapies with the healthcare team to ensure they are safe and appropriate for the individual.

Beyond specific therapies, lifestyle modifications can also contribute to pain management. Maintaining a healthy weight, engaging in regular gentle exercise (as advised by the healthcare team), and getting enough sleep can all play a role in reducing pain and improving overall well-being. Nutritional considerations are also important, as a balanced diet can support the body's healing process and reduce inflammation.

Finally, emotional and psychological support is crucial for effective pain management. Pain can be exacerbated by stress, anxiety, and depression, so addressing these emotional factors can be essential. Counseling, support groups, and other forms of emotional support can help patients develop coping mechanisms and improve their overall quality of life.

In conclusion, managing pain in breast cancer patients requires a comprehensive and individualized approach. Open communication between the patient and their healthcare team is essential for developing an effective pain management plan. By combining pharmacological and non-pharmacological strategies, addressing emotional and psychological factors, and incorporating lifestyle modifications, breast cancer patients can effectively manage their pain and improve their quality of life throughout their cancer journey.(Pain in Cancer Survivors | Journal of Clinical Oncology - ASCO Publications ascopubs.org, Pain associated with breast cancer: etiologies and therapies - PMC - PubMed Central pmc.ncbi.nlm.nih.gov Pain Management in Breast Cancer Patients: A Multidisciplinary Approach - PMC)

Hot Flashes - I sometimes get hot flashes during the day. It feels like the heat is radiating from my ears up to my forehead, and I'm the only one feeling it. My head, whether bald or with thin hair, gets soaked during these episodes. My hot flashes also happen at night, and I literally soak through my sheets.

To deal with this, I wear a bonnet to bed and sleep on or under a bunch of "Fluffies." These are super soft, plush blankets you can find at Walmart or Amazon by searching for "fluffy blankets." They've been a lifesaver! I have one my little sister gave me to support my fight against breast cancer, and I take it with me on infusion days because hospitals and cancer centers are usually cold. While they offer warm blankets for my legs and feet during infusions, it's comforting to have something soft and cuddly that smells like home. The Fluffies create a barrier between my night sweats and the sheets. Some people might prefer a towel. I've also found that jersey knit sheets in the summer and flannel sheets in the winter help. When my night sweats became too much, my oncologist prescribed Clonidine.

Dehydration - Staying hydrated is absolutely crucial, especially during cancer treatment. The medications used are highly toxic, and your body works hard to flush out the chemical byproducts through the endocrine and lymphatic systems, eventually eliminating them in your urine. Dehydration puts a significant strain on your body in many ways. Personally, I know I'm dehydrated when my lips are dry and I get lightheaded. My doctor can always tell from my blood work if my kidney output is high, indicating I haven't had enough fluids. I also get fluids during my chemo treatments to ensure I'm properly hydrated.

Cancercenter.org emphasizes the critical importance of hydration for cancer patients for several reasons: It helps flush out toxins from chemotherapy, lessens side effects like nausea, weakness, constipation, and fatigue, and is even required for the safe administration of some chemotherapy drugs. Dehydration can disrupt your treatment plan. Cancer patients are often advised to drink at least 64 ounces of fluid daily, though individual needs and treatment plans may require more.

Constipation - Let's be real. Dealing with breast cancer is a lot. Between treatments, appointments, and just trying to navigate daily life, the last thing you need is constipation. Unfortunately, it's a pretty common side effect for many breast cancer patients, and it can really add insult to injury. Whether it's from the chemo, pain meds, or even just changes in your routine, a backed-up gut can make an already tough situation even worse.

So, what's a person to do? First off, don't be shy about talking to your doctor. They've heard it all before, and they can offer personalized advice. They might suggest stool softeners, laxatives, or other medications to get things moving again. But it's not just about popping pills. There are some lifestyle tweaks that can make a big difference, too.

Drinking plenty of water is key. Seriously, aim for those 8 glasses a day, or even more if you can. Think of it as flushing out your system. Fiber is your friend, too. Load up on fruits, veggies, and whole grains. They're like little scrub brushes for your intestines. And while you might not feel like it, gentle exercise can help get things moving. Even a short walk can make a difference.

It's also worth paying attention to your body's signals. When you gotta go, you gotta go. Don't put it off. And try to establish a regular bathroom routine. Sometimes just sitting on the toilet at the same time each day can train your body to cooperate.

Dealing with constipation during breast cancer treatment is definitely a pain, but it's something you can manage. Talk to your doctor, make some changes to your diet and lifestyle, and you can get things back on track. Remember, you're not alone in this, and there are ways to feel better.

Treatment medications are drying overall. It flows along with keeping yourself hydrated to stave off constipation. I maintain a daily regimen of 8 to 10 glasses of water daily. I also take a daily fiber supplement from Metamucil. I also take a stool softener daily called Colace. (Constipation and Cancer - Side Effects - NCI www.cancer.gov, Bowel Retraining: Purpose, Procedure, and Risks - Healthline www.healthline.com)

Weird taste - I was warned that my taste buds would change. I was not exactly sure what they meant by that but I can say the first thing to change about my taste was the fact that I can no longer tolerate spicy foods. One of my favorites was Chipotle. I couldn't eat anything on the menu. Everything put my mouth on fire then the second thing to happen was certain foods upon eating them would make me sick and nauseous. For instance, I can no longer eat soggy broccoli. My vegetables have to be al dente. I did not have a taste for vegetables like string beans, Brussels sprouts, or beans (whose texture started to gross me out), but I started to crave cabbage, collard greens, and kale. The meat category became very funny for me as well. My cancer was an ER-positive strain, which means it fed off of estrogen. Foods that contain soy made out of soy and soy-based products I couldn't eat and still do not. I could taste standard meats like chicken, roast beef, and pork chops. It's really weird. I can taste a baked potato but can't taste mashed potatoes. Everything was super salty, too, so I stopped adding salt to my food.

Retinal hemorrhage - A retinal hemorrhage is the term for bleeding in your retina. It comes from a damaged blood vessel. Mine is caused by underlying medical conditions exacerbated by chemotherapy. Hemorrhages are classified by where they develop. I have an actual tear in the tissue of my retina, so it's called an intraretinal hemorrhage. The most noticeable symptom was my vision in my right eye one morning on my way to work. It freaked me out because I know I fought hypertension for a very long time. It was like looking out a kaleidoscope.

Hypertension, or high blood pressure, is a common condition that can affect many parts of the body, including the eyes. One potential consequence of uncontrolled hypertension is retinal hemorrhage, which is bleeding in the retina, the light-sensitive tissue at the back of the eye.

Causes of Retinal Hemorrhage in Hypertensive Patients

High blood pressure can damage the delicate blood vessels in the retina, making them more prone to leakage and bleeding. This can lead to the formation of small, dot-like hemorrhages or larger, flame-shaped hemorrhages in the retina.

Symptoms of Retinal Hemorrhage

In many cases, retinal hemorrhage does not cause any noticeable symptoms. However, if the bleeding is severe or affects the central part of the retina, it can lead to blurred vision, floaters, or even vision loss.

Diagnosis and Treatment

Retinal hemorrhage is usually diagnosed during an eye exam when the doctor can see the bleeding in the retina. Treatment for retinal hemorrhage typically focuses on controlling the underlying hypertension. This may involve lifestyle changes, such as diet and exercise, as well as medication to lower blood pressure. In some cases, laser treatment may be used to seal off leaking blood vessels in the retina.

Prevention of Retinal Hemorrhage

The best way to prevent retinal hemorrhage is to control blood pressure through regular checkups, healthy lifestyle habits, and medication as prescribed by a doctor. It is also important to have regular eye exams to detect any potential problems early on.

Conclusion

Retinal hemorrhage is a potential complication of uncontrolled hypertension. While it may not always cause symptoms, it can lead to vision problems if left untreated. By managing blood pressure and seeking prompt medical attention for any vision changes, individuals with hypertension can help protect their eye health.(How High Blood Pressure Can Lead to Vision Loss | American Heart Association www.heart.org, Hypertensive Retinopathy - Eye Disorders - Merck Manual Professional Edition www.merckmanuals.com, High blood pressure and eye disease Information | Mount Sinai - New York www.mountsinai.org, Hypertensive Retinopathy - StatPearls - NCBI Bookshelf www.ncbi.nlm.nih.gov, Retinal Bleeding: Symptoms, Causes, Diagnosis, and Treatment - Healthlinewww.healthline.com)

Insomnia - Insomnia is defined as habitual sleeplessness, basically the inability to sleep. Insomnia: A Sleep Thief for Chemotherapy Patients

Insomnia, the persistent difficulty falling asleep or staying asleep, is a common and frustrating side effect for many undergoing chemotherapy. This sleep disturbance can significantly impact a patient's quality of life, exacerbating fatigue, mood changes, and overall well-being.

The causes of insomnia in chemotherapy patients are multifaceted. The treatment itself can disrupt sleep patterns due to the powerful drugs circulating in the body. These drugs can interfere with the production of sleep-regulating hormones and neurotransmitters. Additionally, the side effects of chemotherapy, such as nausea, vomiting, pain, and hot flashes, can make it difficult to get comfortable and rest.

Psychological factors also play a significant role. The stress and anxiety associated with a cancer diagnosis and treatment can lead to racing thoughts and worries that keep patients awake at night. Fear of the unknown, concerns about the future, and emotional distress can all contribute to insomnia.

Fortunately, there are strategies to manage insomnia during chemotherapy. It's crucial to maintain a consistent sleep schedule, going to bed and waking up at the same time each day, even on weekends. Creating a relaxing bedtime routine, such as taking a warm bath, reading a book, or listening to calming music, can help prepare the body for sleep. The bedroom environment should be conducive to sleep, dark, quiet, and cool.

It's also important to avoid caffeine and alcohol before bed, as these substances can interfere with sleep. Regular exercise can improve sleep quality, but it's best to avoid intense physical activity close to bedtime. If sleep doesn't come within 20 minutes of lying down, it's recommended to get out of bed and do a relaxing activity until feeling tired.

In some cases, medical interventions may be necessary. Doctors may prescribe sleep medications to help patients get the rest they need. Cognitive behavioral therapy for insomnia (CBT-I) is a type of therapy that can help patients identify and change negative thoughts and behaviors that contribute to insomnia. Relaxation techniques, such as deep breathing exercises and meditation, can also be helpful.

Insomnia can be a challenging aspect of chemotherapy treatment, but it's not something patients have to endure in silence. By working with their healthcare team and implementing various strategies, patients can improve their sleep quality and overall well-being during this difficult time.

I find that this happens usually on the day that I get chemotherapy. I am up in the middle of the night and early morning hours with the inability to rest. There are a few things that I do to combat this I love tea. There is one night time blend that I prefer over just basic chamomile tea. It’s called Sleepytime Tea by Celestial Seasonings. It comes in a box with a little teddy bear on it and his pajamas, and it is the best hot. Although you could drink it cold if you prefer, the effects are still the same. There was also a cocoa That came from a company called Ryze. It is made out of mushrooms and contains melatonin. I will put on Pink noise or white noise and watch sermons on YouTube. I love to watch sermons by Micheal Todd, Jackie Hill Perry, Sarah Jakes Roberts, or Stephanie OkaforIf all else failed, I would definitely fall asleep reading my Bible. (Sleep Problems in People with Cancer - Side Effects - NCI www.cancer.gov, Anxiety and sleep disorders in cancer patients - PMC pmc.ncbi.nlm.nih.gov, Difficulty sleeping (insomnia) and cancer www.cancerresearchuk.org, Mechanisms of Chemotherapy-Induced Neurotoxicity - PMC - PubMed Centralpmc.ncbi.nlm.nih.gov, Sleeping Well | Cancer Survivors - CDCwww.cdc.gov)

Dark Nail Beds- The side effects are troubling at all levels, but they do differ in intensity, duration, and occurrence. There is no forewarning or ramp-up to my symptoms. They just hit, and that could be a singular occurrence or multiple symptoms one or more times a day. As an adult, you are used to having control over yourself and your situations. As an adult you usually play a major role in the plans for how things will happen. But when you have cancer, you lose that control, and you cannot predict the results. That is the part that sucks.

When my cancer recurred, I was put on a new chemotherapy regimen, this time including an immunology injection 24 hours later. I had my port reinstalled because my veins couldn't take the burning from the Gemcitabine. This transfusion of medication going through my veins in my arm was starting to scar. The name of my new chemotherapy drug is a combination of Carboplatin and Gemcitabine known as GemCarbo.

Neulasta (pegfilgrastim) is a medication used to stimulate the growth of white blood cells, specifically neutrophils. It is commonly used in patients undergoing chemotherapy, as chemotherapy can significantly suppress the bone marrow's ability to produce these infection-fighting cells. By boosting neutrophil production, Neulasta helps reduce the risk of infection, a serious and potentially life-threatening complication of chemotherapy.

Neulasta is a long-acting form of granulocyte colony-stimulating factor (G-CSF). It is administered as a single injection, typically 24 hours after chemotherapy. While Neulasta is effective in preventing infections, it can also cause a range of side effects, some of which can be significant.

One of the most common side effects of Neulasta is bone pain. This pain, often described as a deep ache in the bones, is usually mild to moderate but can be severe in some cases. It occurs because Neulasta stimulates the bone marrow to produce neutrophils, and this increased activity can cause discomfort. Over-the-counter pain relievers, such as ibuprofen or acetaminophen, are often used to manage this side effect.

Another common side effect is injection site reactions. These reactions can include redness, swelling, pain, or itching at the injection site. These reactions are usually mild and resolve on their own within a few days. Applying a cold compress to the injection site can help alleviate discomfort.

Less common but more serious side effects include allergic reactions. These reactions can range from mild rash and itching to severe anaphylaxis, a life-threatening condition that requires immediate medical attention. Signs of an allergic reaction include hives, difficulty breathing, swelling of the face, lips, or tongue, and chest pain.

Neulasta can also cause a rare but serious condition called acute febrile neutrophilic dermatosis (Sweet's syndrome). This condition is characterized by fever, painful skin lesions, and an elevated white blood cell count. It requires prompt medical treatment.

In some cases, Neulasta can affect the spleen, causing it to enlarge. Splenic rupture, although rare, is a serious complication that requires emergency surgery. Symptoms of splenic rupture include left upper abdominal pain, shoulder pain, and dizziness.

It is important to note that this is not an exhaustive list of all possible side effects. Patients should discuss the potential risks and benefits of Neulasta with their healthcare provider before starting treatment. Regular monitoring and communication with the healthcare team are essential to manage any side effects that may occur.

In conclusion, Neulasta is a valuable medication for preventing infections in patients undergoing chemotherapy. However, it can cause various side effects, some of which can be serious. Patients should be aware of these potential side effects and report any unusual symptoms to their healthcare provider promptly. Careful consideration of the risks and benefits of Neulasta is essential to ensure safe and effective treatment. (healthqueue.netNeulasta | European Medicines Agency (EMA) www.ema.europa.eu,

Trajectory of absolute neutrophil counts in patients treated with pegfilgrastim on the day of chemotherapy versus the day after chemotherapy pmc.ncbi.nlm.nih.gov)

Surgery

I elected to have a lumpectomy. Mayoclinic.com describes a lumpectomy as a surgical procedure used in the treatment of breast cancer. It involves the removal of the tumor and a small margin of surrounding healthy tissue while conserving a large amount of the breast tissue itself. The main goal of this surgery is to eliminate the cancerous cells from the breast in one swoop. My surgeon made an incision and removed the tumor along with a rim of normal tissue in pursuit of what she called "clear margins. The margins were defined by the placement of these long wires that stuck out of my breast like antennas. The whole scenario reminded me of a sci-fi movie where the main character is trying to contact Mars. Judging by the looks of my boob, we should've gotten some good reception. It was done under full anesthesia, so I was only up to experience that for a little bit. I woke up three hours later not feeling anything in my left breast but woozy from the anesthesia, and according to my doctors and my nurses, there was no message from Mars.

I recently had my second surgery and am recovering as I finish this book. I wasn't nearly as nervous this time. This surgery involved both a breast surgeon and a plastic surgeon. Dr. Williams removed 9mm of residual tumor, scar tissue from my previous surgery, and a microchip left from the last lumpectomy. Dr. Patel closed the incision on my left breast and performed a symmetry procedure on my right breast to match the size of the left. The incision was glued closed to minimize scarring and create smooth lines. It's hard to even tell I had surgery. I wonder if this is how women feel after breast augmentation. Everything went as planned, thankfully. I was under anesthesia for about three hours. I was a little woozy waking up, but I had no nausea or pain and was able to go home the same day. Now I'm home recovering with basic wound care. I should be fully recovered in about four weeks. ***Shout out to the wonderful staff at Fox Chase Cancer Center in Philadelphia, PA. They are the bestest!***

Radiation

Radiation therapy consisted of 23 active sessions of proton therapy. It is a type of radiation therapy that is targeted more so than traditional radiation therapy. It uses high-intensity energy beams to destroy the cancer cells. The benefit is that it can destroy cancer cells within a specific targeted area with little effect on the surrounding healthy tissue. (medline.com)

I was prepared with two separate measuring appointments. I was fitted with an old-fashioned bra and put under the laser, where markings were put in specific increments. I was also tattooed with a little dot on my left breast that lined up with the machine as a reference point for all the other measurements. In the very first session, I spent about 30 minutes getting fitted into that old-fashioned bra apparatus. Then, they marked it with a felt tip pen, putting dashes, arrows, and lines. The second session was a bit longer. About 40 minutes was spent lying atop the table with the actual laser machine hovering over me. The technicians lined each point up with the bra and performed a short trial run of the laser session. The laser sessions themselves don't last very long. I don't believe I was ever on the table longer than 20 minutes. It is the preparation for your laser therapy sessions that takes up the most amount of your time.

GIANTS/Slayers

GIANTS

Are GIANTS real? The Cambridge Dictionary defines "GIANT" as an imaginary or mythological being of human form but superhuman size and strength. It also uses "GIANT" as an adjective, describing something of very great size or force, like a gigantic wave. GIANTS are often portrayed as extremely tall, strong, and usually very cruel. Think big, strong, and mean.

GIANTS are huge beings from folklore, taller than buildings, reaching the clouds. They're extraordinarily strong, able to move things much bigger than themselves. They can be nice or mean despite their scary appearance. They have large, human-like features—big eyes, loud voices, and huge hands.

People fear GIANTS because of their size and strength, which can make them feel small and weak. GIANTS can cause trouble, intentionally or accidentally, due to their sheer size, making them seem dangerous. But not all GIANTS are bad; some can be seen as motivational. It's all about perspective. Fear often comes from the unknown and what could happen, not the GIANTS themselves.

GIANTS are, well, gigantic. That's why we use "GIANT" as an adjective, too, like "that's a GIANT building" or "that's a GIANT amount of money." When facing a GIANT, you might feel like you're going to lose. Let's talk about my favorite GIANT story: David and Goliath.

Picture this: Vacation Bible School at Zion Hill Baptist Church, filled with Bible stories, arts and crafts, and churned ice cream. You know why I love Chick-fil-A? Their Ice Dream tastes exactly like that ice cream Deacon Walthour and Deacon Bowman used to make! (Sidebar: the fact that such a heavenly treat comes from a Christian establishment proves there's a God, right? It even tastes good during chemo! Heaven on earth. I loved it, and the fact that it's a Christian-run business further confirms God's existence to me.) Here's a tip: always remember to enjoy the little things that bring you joy. They matter.

I watched a sermon by Micheal Todd that spoke about receipts being used as proof of purchase/existence. I had a thought rather, a question popped into my mind, is there actual proof of GIANTS?

The enduring fascination with GIANTS has permeated human cultures for millennia, giving rise to countless myths, legends, and folklore. From the towering Goliath in biblical texts to the monstrous cyclops of Greek mythology, the idea of beings of extraordinary size and strength has captured our imaginations. Yet, despite this rich cultural history, concrete scientific evidence for the existence of GIANTS remains elusive.

The search for proof of GIANTS often focuses on archaeological discoveries. Occasionally, unusually large bones are unearthed, sparking excitement and speculation. However, these finds are often attributed to known species of megafauna, such as mammoths or large dinosaurs. While some argue that these remains could be evidence of undiscovered GIANT hominids, the scientific community generally requires more substantial and conclusive proof. Skeletal remains attributed to GIANTS often turn out to be misidentified or misassembled bones from multiple individuals or different species.

Another area of interest lies in the numerous accounts of GIANT skeletons and artifacts reported throughout history. These reports, often found in local newspapers or historical records, frequently lack verifiable evidence. Many such claims have been debunked through further investigation, revealing hoaxes, misinterpretations, or outright fabrications. The lack of proper documentation, scientific analysis, and contextual information makes it difficult to assess the validity of these claims.

Proponents of the existence of GIANTS sometimes point to megalithic structures, such as Stonehenge or the pyramids of Giza, as evidence of GIANT builders. The sheer size and complexity of these monuments, they argue, could only have been achieved with the help of beings possessing superhuman strength. However, mainstream archaeology offers alternative explanations for the construction of these structures, focusing on the ingenuity and organizational skills of ancient civilizations. While these explanations may not fully account for every aspect of these impressive feats of engineering, they do not necessitate the existence of GIANTS.

In conclusion, while the concept of GIANTS continues to fascinate, scientific proof remains lacking. Archaeological discoveries, historical accounts, and megalithic structures have all been cited as potential evidence, but these claims have yet to withstand rigorous scientific scrutiny. Until more substantial and verifiable evidence is unearthed, the existence of GIANTS will likely remain firmly in the realm of myth and legend. (Fact or Fiction: Did GIANTS Once Roam the Earth? | 01 - Vocal Media vocal.media, Archaeological Evidence for GIANTS in the Bible? - YouTube www.youtube.com ,Greek GIANTS | AMNHwww.amnh.org)

The Valley of Elah lies between King Saul's palace to the north and the Philistine camp to the south—kind of like a North Philly versus South Philly rivalry. It's about 15 miles west of Bethlehem and 20 miles east of the Mediterranean Sea, which sounds a lot like the Philly suburbs, maybe around Valley Forge.

The Philistines were a Canaanite people who lived in Israel before the Israelites arrived. The Israelites couldn't conquer them, and the two nations fought for much of Israel's history. The Philistine stronghold was on the coastal plain in the Gaza area. They were a powerful, technologically advanced culture, possessing iron and doing everything they could to prevent Israel from accessing it. They worshipped false gods, the two most important being Baal and Dagon.

Goliath and the Philistine army were trying to advance through the Valley of Elah toward the heart of Judea. King Saul and his army met them there to stop them. It was going to be an epic, winner-take-all battle, with the loser serving the winner. So, basically, Goliath was on his way to conquer the region, but he holed up outside of King of Prussia in Valley Forge to fight. (holylandsite.com)

The Israelites and the Philistines are about to rumble. I feel like it was WWEish, with announcers saying, " LET'S GET READY TO RUMMMMMBBBLLE!!!!" King Saul and his army are lined up on one side and the Philistines on the other, a valley between them. This would be a match of all times, sort of like the Super Bowl. I'm sure a battle of this magnitude would be televised with people throwing parties and grilling in our times, or would it look more like the war-torn images sent to us from other countries battling for their freedom?

Now, during this time, David was just a young boy. His father sent him out to the battlefield to take his brother's lunch. He just happened upon the whole situation with Goliath big behind talking smack about the Israelites and blaspheming God. At first, David was asking about what was going on, and the soldiers were "scuurrred". Then he asked his brother, who basically led him. David was too young to be in the army. His brothers were brushing him off, talking about him being too young. Army and was a little thing, according to the stories I'm told. Just the fact Goliathu was so full of himself that he actually laughed and scoffed at David. He thought this kid was a joke and an insult. Big mistake. David would go on and quickly rise to prominence when he defeated Goliath with just a sling and a stone. He stood up to a GIANT of a man with a mere stone and a sling! Scene change: the camera zooms in on Goliath standing there in full battle gear. It starts at his feet and slowly pans up his legs, covered in shields. Slowly, the camera pans up to this

9ft 6 in man unveiling a sheath girded around his loin, full chest plate, and the true meaning of an armor bearer was with him. So, in reality, it was two people standing up to David. See how the odds were stacked against this kid. Everything about this beef is off. I was also thinking that they didn't have deodorant back then. Goliath had been out there talking smack in the valley for days. I'm sure his big behind was stinking, so ewww. This big ole stinking dude is the supposed champion of the Philistines. Boo, and again, I say Boo. The next thing I knew, David had done Oops upside the head with this smooth stone, and the fight was ova! Do you hear me? Finished Goliath was D- E- A- D. Dead hunnti. This victory immediately threw David into the limelight. He became a close advisor to King Saul, and after Saul's death, David was anointed as the new king of Israel. Now you see how the underdog in this situation persevered against the GIANT in his life? This is how we have to go about fighting cancer as if we're the David, and we're the meek and the small one in this situation, and breast cancer is the big old Goliath trying to take over our territory and our bodies.

As I said, Jesse sent David out to the field with a quart of roasted rice and ten loaves of bread for his three oldest brothers, Eliab, Abinadab, and Shammah, and ten wedges of cheese for their commander's lunch. Jesse told him to check on the status of the fight and to bring back word that his brothers were cool. This wasn't just a walk around the corner; the valley was out past where David tended sheep in Bethlehem. Put one group on the east side of Valley Forge and the other on the west side. David is coming from Philly. David comes off the I-76 exit and sees headquarters set up at Valley

Casino. David did this for 40 days. Goliath is talking mad smack on the field for 40 days, day and night." Yooooo, y'all Israelites ain't ***t! We are from Gath! GATH SIIIIIIDE! GATH GANG GANG! I know y'all not 'bout to step to me, the Philistine champion? Are y'all lining up to fight? Y'all Saul's peeps, right?! Send one of you, anyone will do. If they can beat and kill me, we will be your servants. But, If I kill them, you will be our slaves... Send me SOMEBODY, and we will FIGHT!" King Saul is petrified and issues his own declaration. Saul replies, "Any man that defeats this man, I'll make him rich, give him my daughter to marry, and their household will no longer have to pay taxes." Right when David is asking the front line commanders about his brother, she overhears Goliath talking smack, sees that the Israelites are backing away terrified, and hears the cowering soldiers whispering about the king's reward. So David asks, "What's up with this uncircumcised Philistine? Who is this dude to insult the army of the living God? What happens to the man that defeats him?". Eliab, David's oldest brother, overheard him talking to the soldiers about Saul's reward and got upset. "Why are you down here?! Who's watching your sheep?! You're just being nosey!" he barked at his little brother. "What did I do?! I was just asking a question. ", David replied. So David turned and asked somebody else the same thing and got the same reply.

Saul, holed up in the Valley of Elah (the Israelite army headquarters), overheard David talking about Goliath and what was happening. He sent for David, who told Saul not to be afraid and that he would fight Goliath. Saul scoffed, saying David was just a boy while Goliath had been a warrior since his youth. David countered, explaining how he'd defended his father's sheep from lions and bears, even killing them. He argued that this "uncircumcised Philistine" was no different, having insulted the army of the living God. "God rescued me from those lions and bears," David said, "and He'll rescue me from this Philistine."

Saul relented, telling David to go and that God would be with him. But then he tried to dress David in his own armor and helmet and gave him a sword. David, who'd never worn armor, couldn't even walk in it. He took it all off, grabbed five smooth stones from the stream bed, put them in his shepherd's bag, and, with his sling, went out to face Goliath.

As Goliath approached, his shield-bearer in front, he sneered at David, seeing only a boy. Goliath was insulted that David would dare fight him. "Am I a joke to you?" he asked. David retorted, "You come at me with a sword, a spear, and a curved blade, but I come at you in the name of the Lord! Today, you're getting your tail whooped. I'm going to cut off your head and feed your body to the wild animals. Then, the whole world will know that God is on Israel's side and doesn't need a spear or sword. He owns this war!"

Goliath moved closer to attack. David ran toward the front lines, reached into his bag, took out a stone, and KA-WIKKITT!—hit Goliath smack-dab in the forehead. Goliath fell dead on the spot. That's how David slew Goliath, the GIANT!

King David, the shepherd, poet, and warrior king of Israel, had a complex and vibrant prayer life. His prayers, as recorded in the

Psalms, are a testament to his deep relationship with God and offer insights into his joys, sorrows, triumphs, and struggles.

David's prayers were characterized by a wide range of emotions and expressions. He praised God for his steadfast love and faithfulness, as seen in Psalm 103: "Bless the Lord, O my soul, and all that is within me, bless his holy name!" He also cried out to God in times of distress and despair, as in Psalm 22: "My God, my God, why have you forsaken me?"

His prayers were not limited to personal matters. He intercedes for his people, as in Psalm 51, where he pleads for God's mercy on Israel after his sin with Bathsheba. He also prayed for his enemies, asking God to turn their hearts or bring justice, as seen in Psalm 109.

David's prayer life was marked by consistency and devotion. He prayed regularly, as mentioned in Psalm 55:17: "Evening and morning and at noon I utter my complaint and groan, and he hears my voice." He also sought God's guidance in every aspect of his life, from battles to personal decisions.

One of the most striking aspects of David's prayers is his honesty and vulnerability. He laid his heart bare before God, expressing his doubts, fears, and regrets. In Psalm 51, he confesses his sin and pleads for forgiveness: "Have mercy on me, O God, according to your steadfast love; according to the abundance of your mercies, blot out my transgressions."

David's prayers were not just words; they were a reflection of his deep trust in God. He believed that God heard his prayers and would answer them according to his will. This faith sustained him through trials and tribulations, and it is evident in his words in Psalm 27:14: "Wait for the Lord; be strong, and let your heart take courage; wait for the Lord!"

In conclusion, King David's prayer life was a tapestry of praise, lament, intercession, and confession. His prayers reveal a man who was deeply devoted to God, honest in his dealings with him, and confident in his love and faithfulness. David's prayers continue to inspire and challenge us to cultivate a deeper relationship with God through prayer. (www.inearthenvessels.com, David and the Power of Prayer – YouTube www.youtube.com, King David's Prayers: Deep, Complex, and Relevant Today - Join The Journey www.jointhejourney.com)

Slayers

A GIANT Slayer is a person who conquers a GIANT. In our case, those of us battling breast cancer conquer GIANTS daily. I want to shine a light on accomplishments because it is necessary for our total healing. I want to encourage you and the fact that the GIANTS that we face in our separate journeys can be defeated. They can be conquered. Cancer does not have to rule our lives. We can beat this thing and put forth a valiant effort in doing so. Let me highlight a couple of GIANT slayers that particularly caught my eye.

The tale of Jack and the Beanstalk at night, where I learned about a “GIANT slayer.” She would change her voice to sound like the GIANT, loud and booming. In my mind, I was thinking Jack better get his **** out of there. I thought this kid would be devoured. The story is about Jack, a boy who lives on a farm with his mom. They run out of food, and she tells Jack to go to the town square and exchange the cow for food. At the market, Jack falls for a scam by a man who sells him magic beans. Jack gives up the family cow for the beans. When Jack gets home with the beans, his mother is angry. She throws the beans out of Jack's hand onto the ground and scolds him harshly because they have no food left. During the night, as Jack sleeps, the beans grow into huge vines that reach high up into the sky. Jack's curiosity was aroused when he saw the Beanstalk after waking up. He climbed it to see where it would take him. At the top of the Beanstalk, he spotted a distant Kingdom that he approached and entered. Everything in this Kingdom was enormous. He went inside the castle. Jack finds a goose in a cage in the castle's kitchen. He hears a GIANT say, "Fee fi fo fum, I smell the blood of an Englishman. The GIANT looks for Jack, who escapes with the goose that lays golden eggs. The GIANT pursues him. Jack hurries back and descends the Beanstalk quickly. Jack cuts down the Beanstalk and makes the GIANT fall to his death. Jack goes home with the goose that lays golden eggs, rescues his family from hunger, and takes care of them forever.

I think Jack is a hero who got revenge for his father's death, reclaimed the family wealth, and added more from the goose. He also protected his mother and their future. That sounds like a win, no?

1) Jack needed some kind of faith to exchange his family's most valuable possession, that cow, for some magic beans. My mother would have been furious with me if I had done something like that.

2) He had to take a risk and trust someone he did not know. He did not know if those beans were really magic or not.

3) There is an element of revenge and victory in his GIANT because he gets the opportunity to reclaim the coins that were originally taken by the GIANT from his father and get justice for his father's death.

4) There is a lot of discussion about the morality of stealing in this story. In some of the adaptations, there is a goose that lays golden eggs. But was it really stealing? This GIANT killed Jack's father. He took gold coins from him. He and his mother were almost

starving. In today's court, I think Jack would be seen as acting in self-defense. He flies on the bird back down the beanstalk, chops that thing down, and kills the GIANT. That part, right?!

"Fee, fi, fo, fum! I smell the blood of an Englishman!" The GIANT's booming pronouncements in "Jack and the Beanstalk" are familiar to many, but beyond the fantastical elements of magic beans and towering beanstalks, the story offers a rich ground for exploring various life lessons. While often categorized as a simple children's tale, "Jack and the Beanstalk" presents complex themes of courage, resourcefulness, consequences, and the ambiguous nature of right and wrong.

One of the most prominent lessons is the importance of courage and taking risks. Jack's initial decision to trade the family cow for magic beans, though seemingly foolish, demonstrates a willingness to step outside the ordinary. This act, driven by desperation and a glimmer of hope, sets him on a path fraught with danger but ultimately leads to a better life. His subsequent climbs up the beanstalk, each time facing the terrifying GIANT, reinforce this theme of courage in the face of adversity. Without his willingness to take these risks, Jack would never have discovered the GIANT's riches or freed himself and his mother from poverty.

Resourcefulness is another key takeaway. Jack isn't physically strong or particularly clever in the traditional sense. However, he possesses practical intelligence and an ability to think on his feet. He uses his cunning to outsmart the GIANT, stealing his treasures and escaping his wrath. His resourcefulness is exemplified by his quick thinking in chopping down the beanstalk, preventing the GIANT's descent. The story highlights the value of adaptability and making the most of limited resources, emphasizing that intelligence isn't always about academic knowledge but also about practical problem-solving.

The story also explores the complex issue of consequences. Jack's actions, while ultimately beneficial to him and his family, are not without their repercussions. He steals from the GIANT, an act that, while portrayed as justifiable given the GIANT's nature, still carries moral weight. The GIANT's pursuit and eventual demise, though presented as a victory for Jack, underscore the potential dangers of impulsive actions and the ripple effects they can have. The narrative prompts reflection on the ethical dimensions of achieving one's goals, suggesting that even in desperate circumstances, actions have consequences.

Finally, "Jack and the Beanstalk" raises questions about the nature of good and evil. The GIANT is undoubtedly a terrifying figure, but he is also presented as the owner of the stolen treasures. Jack's actions, while motivated by need, can be viewed as theft. The story challenges the reader to consider the perspectives of both characters and to recognize the moral ambiguities inherent in the situation. It avoids simplistic categorizations of good and evil, instead presenting a more nuanced view where the lines between right and wrong are blurred.

In conclusion, "Jack and the Beanstalk" is more than just a fantastical adventure. It's a story that explores themes of courage, resourcefulness, consequences, and the complexities of morality. Through Jack's journey up the beanstalk, the story offers valuable lessons about taking calculated risks, utilizing one's abilities, understanding the impact of actions, and recognizing the often-ambiguous nature of right and wrong. These lessons, woven into the fabric of a captivating narrative, continue to resonate with audiences of all ages, making "Jack and the Beanstalk" a timeless and enduring tale.

In my mind, Jack is a hero, in this case, avenging his father's death, recovering the family wealth, and increasing from the goose for generational wealth. Add to that the fact that he saved his mother’s life and secured the future. I would say that was a win, right? You betta slay Jack!

Angels

And the Angel of the Lord told me, "You Elect One, the world will witness the glory of the Lord through you. Write your name in the hidden language behind your right ear. " I had a vision of Michael, my Archangel, who protects me because of my position in the spiritual world. You know angels have ranks in the heavens. Higher-ranking angels have greater power and authority than lower ones, and different ranks look different. (Wikipedia. org) The Assumption of the Virgin painting by Francesco Botticini (1475-75) shows three hierarchies and nine orders, each with its own characteristics. They are put in orders by function and hierarchies by rank. Micheal is an archangel. Michael is the chief of angels and archangels and he's the guardian of the Prince of Israel and is responsible for the care of Israel. Michael is the Angel they talked about in Revelations who does battle with Satan and throws him out of heaven so he no longer has access to God. (Green, Gene (2008) Jude and 2 Peters. Baker. Isbn 9780801026720)

I was struck by the realization that God had created this magnificent being. Jeremiah 1:5 says, "Before I formed you in the womb I knew you; before you were born I set you apart; I appointed you as a prophet to the nations." This understanding reinforces why this particular angel is with me.

Let me try to describe him. The first thing I always notice is his wings. Imagine the softest goose feather, its edges glimmering with gold in the light. Now, picture feathers that are iridescent and practically glowing. Enlarge it drastically, like the huge ostrich feathers used for arrows or in theatrical costumes. Now, in your mind's eye, picture two of these massive, opulent, stark white wings. He's so bright. It's like a dazzlingly white commercial.

He is a brown-skinned angel, his skin also possessing that inner glimmer. It's a bright, pulsing glow, like a heartbeat. Often, when he appears, he's so radiant I can barely look at him, even in my dreams. I suppose that's what it's like coming from the presence of the Most Holy King of Kings, the Lord of Lords. Sometimes, I can see his face, but the details are unclear. However, I can always see three things, regardless of his wings or the intensity of his glow: his huge size, his marvelous wings, and the kindest eyes imaginable.

The first time I noticed him, I was working for this staffing company in Delaware County. It was two days after 911, and I had just returned to work. I was sitting stewing over the reprimand I just received. I saw movement out of the corner of my eye in the office. I didn't see it anymore. Then I saw this flapping movement up and down like a bird in flight. These beautiful big, huge white wings appeared out of nowhere, and the voice said do not fear the Lord thy God is with you couldn't see his face because the huge wings were covering it, and their feet were like a mist dress and white robes with a gold belt draped around his waist folded and flowing this Angel basically stayed in my ear as I drove to pick the kids up from daycare and has appeared to me ever since with messages or instructions from the Lord if Michael brings the messages it is pressing urgently.

I met my angel while working at a small, stressful staffing agency in the Philadelphia suburbs. My boss was rude and seemed threatened by my continuing education, constantly criticizing me. As a young, single mother of two, I was struggling. Inspired by T.D. Jakes and Juanita Bynum, I prayed for help one night. I wondered if what I was about to see was real or just my imagination.

"Be still and know that He is God," I heard in my mind. Then, I saw him. He was an angel, ten feet tall, twice my size, and radiating light. He appeared human-like, wearing a flowing, opalescent white robe, a gleaming gold sash, and a magnificent sword adorned with jewels and unfamiliar script. The sword was intricately detailed and inscribed with an ancient language. The light emanating from within him was so intense it was as if he had his own spotlight.

Scanning him from head to toe, I couldn't discern if he had hair. Around his head was a ring of pure brightness, not a distinct object, but an aura. Below that were his majestic, enormous wings. They resembled ostrich feathers but bleached a perfect white, sprinkled with what looked like shimmering dust, and lit from behind, giving them a soft glow. The very tips of each feather were gilded in gold, like the gilded edges of some Bibles that gleam when closed. His wingspan was immense, the feathers flowing from the top of his head all the way to the ground.

In fact, I never saw his feet. They were obscured, so I don't know if he wore shoes or sandals. He simply hovered. His robes flowed and swayed as if in a breeze. His very presence commanded attention. He was a GIANT of a being. I call him Michael, believing Archangel Michael to be my guardian angel. Given all the challenges I've faced, the times I've been spared, and the ways God has intervened in my life, it feels right.

FEAR

Why not fear cancer?

Oomph! Fear takes on so many different shapes and forms, and it is no different when you hear the word cancer, and they're talking about you. Fear of the unknown is the biggest because each person's cancer journey is so specific to that person. They are commonalities, of course. However, even within those commonalities, there are differences. The genetic makeup of an individual makes it almost impossible to work within finite numbers. You are usually working with percentages and those percentages track common responses to treatment. It is the 1% and 2% less likely, the 5% chances, and the low occurrence of side effects that removed the definite from the equation of available answers. There is no definitive answer to cancer. That leaves open a myriad of questions and plenty of space to worry.

Fear is a feeling we have when we expect or recognize a danger or a threat. It doesn't matter if it's real or not. It can make us feel very bad and prepare us to deal with possible harm. Fear As a response is a natural, powerful, and primitive human emotion that involves an Overall biochemical response as well as a high individual emotional response[2]. Physiologically, it triggers the "fight-or-flight" response, releasing hormones that prepare the body to either stay and fight the threat or to run away to safety[1].

- As a Protective Mechanism: It serves as a survival mechanism, signaling our bodies to respond with defensive actions[2].

The concept of fear is also used in a broader sense to denote reverence or awe, especially toward a deity[1]. It's a complex state that can be both instinctual and learned, varying greatly among individuals and situations[2]. Fear can be immediate, triggered by the presence of danger, or it can be anticipatory, arising from the thought of potential danger or the unknown[1]. (merriam-webster.com, dictionary. com)

Think about it: you don't know what your cancer journey holds. You are unsure of how you will respond to the treatments. In the beginning, you're unsure of what your treatment plan looks like. Whether or not you need surgery, radiation treatments, or how long you'll be at certain stages, have you ever recovered? We have all heard horror stories about pain and sickness, possible disfigurement, and doom and gloom. It is a lot, and sometimes that "a lot" is overwhelming. I hope the words that you find in this book bring you some form of comfort, a peek into the unknown, and some level of understanding of what I have and continue to contend with. May a part of you identify with that part of me that somehow helps. My cancer journey brought up fears that I was aware of and had before I was ever diagnosed, but it also brought up a lot of fears that I didn't even know were there.

A short time after my diagnosis of breast cancer, we had a strong storm that came through Philadelphia. It knocked out the power lines in my neighborhood. We were plunged into pitch-dark blackness. It wasn't a problem at first then suddenly something changed. I got so hot! The air stood motionless but, at the same time, got thicker. The air conditioner was off along with my personal fan.

It was dark, DARK, and I swore I felt something like a wool blanket come over me. I couldn't breathe! My heart was racing. My heart was pounding as if someone was trying to break out the door or break out the walls of my chest! I thought my heart was going to burst right there. I started to tear up. Why on earth was I crying? Then I started crying because I didn't know why I was crying. I still couldn't catch my breath. What is happening? I needed LIGHT! I am scrambling to light the candles I had on my dresser. I was Looking for a lighter or a book of matches in the dark. Finally, it dawned on me, and I turned on the flashlight on my cell phone. Within the glow of these things, I sat and calmed myself. It was a point there where it literally felt like something huge had covered me, and I was just holding on tight until that light came through from my cell phone. It was with that subtle glow and the restoration of electricity about an hour and a half later that I was able to calm myself enough to realize that what I experienced in that storm was a panic attack. Panic is a form of fear.

Mayoclinic.org says: A panic attack is a sudden episode of intense fear that triggers severe physical reactions when there is no real danger or apparent cause. It can be very frightening and overwhelming, often making individuals feel like they're losing control, having a heart attack, or even dying. Ahh, that sounds like me right there…sudden, overwhelming, and about to die. Let me see what else. These attacks begin suddenly and without warning. Panic attacks include symptoms such as:

- a rapid pounding heart rate
- sweating trembling
- shortness of breath
- chills hot flashes
- nausea
- abdominal cramping
- chest pain
- headaches
- dizziness
- numbness

I learned to address my panic attacks with a very simple technique. You can do it to calm yourself in any situation that brings you an unexpected, heightened sense of anxiety or need for awareness or to focus on yourself. Basically, what you do is you breathe in through your nose for four counts, hold for four counts, breathe out through your mouth through pursed lips like you are getting ready to kiss someone for four counts, and hold for four counts. It's really simple. You can adapt this breathing method to whatever suits you best to calm yourself in the moment, but it works.

The Shame of it all

One would think that an uncontrollable illness like cancer would offer some form of comfort because there is nothing that I did to "catch" it. I have no family history of breast cancer on my mother's side. I have no way of knowing about my father or anything about his side, but the BRCA test results were negative for any mutations. BRCA testing in breast cancer is a genetic test that looks for specific mutations in the BRCA1 and BRCA2 genes.

I was embarrassed to have breast cancer at first. What did I do wrong? I was not the healthiest version of myself, but did I eat something or do something to cause this to occur? Where was I exposed to the carcinogen that caused this tumor to grow? How did I not notice an almost 7mm growth? I mean, I did all the breast exams while showering, looking for dimples and puckers. Nothing. Why me, Lord?

The shame surfaced in areas I didn't even remember. I had to ask myself one day when did I start covering myself up in front of my husband? Since when do I wear a robe to go take a shower? I mean, the robe was in the bathroom afterward, but I have never done things like this before. I am a steak down the hallway type of gal because all my stuff is in the room, you know. I realized that, in essence, I was ashamed of my body. My affected breast was still disfigured from the first lumpectomy and is now dark due to radiation. My right breast is "droopy" due to gravity and far less attention. An overall unevenness that I am sure was affecting my gate. Now, after the 2nd surgery, I look somewhat normal, with both of the girls sitting up perkier than ever.

I remember visiting a girlfriend of mine who, at the time, was just informed that her cancer had metastasized to her bones. I thought to myself how powerful of a woman she was, fighting cancer and still managing her children and life. Little did I know I would be in the same boat just one year later, dealing with the challenges of a metastatic life.

I feel so different about breast cancer now. Breast cancer came back as stage 4 in the scar bed from the first tumor removal. It was very aggressive! A small area, the size of a quarter, started to bulge out like a pimple. It hurt so much in my breast for the first time. It looked like a pimple that was raised, hot, itchy, tight, and ready to pop. I was afraid it would burst through the skin. I did not want a hole in my breast. I had to act fast. I also had a tiny glowing spot on my right lung. I had to either biopsy that spot on my lung or agree that I had stage 4 breast cancer that had spread and start treatment. A special doctor who could do the biopsy was hard to find because of the spot's location in my lung. They had to go through my breast and chest wall, not through my throat with a scope. They could have made my lung collapse. The decision to admit that stage of cancer that had spread meant I would always need some form of treatment.

This treatment has caused me to gain soooo much weight. I cannot help but be ashamed of how my body looks during this process. Now, I know most people on chemotherapy worry about losing weight, but I cannot be the only one going through this. So, because this big gut bothered me, I started to research what I could do to assist in my healing process. I read two books, The Mind-Gut Connection by Emeran Mayer, MD, and The Garden Within by Dr. Anita Phillips, and the information contained within blew my mind.

In "The Mind-Gut Connection," Dr. Emeran Mayer explores the fascinating and complex relationship between our minds and our guts. He delves into the scientific evidence that reveals how these two seemingly separate systems are actually deeply intertwined, constantly communicating and influencing each other in profound ways.

Mayer explains that the gut, with its trillions of bacteria, fungi, and other microorganisms (collectively known as the microbiome), is not just a site of digestion but also a crucial player in our overall health and well-being. The gut and its microbiome have a direct line of communication with the brain through neural, hormonal, and immune pathways. This means that changes in the gut can affect our mood, emotions, and even our cognitive functions, and vice versa.

The book highlights how this mind-gut connection plays a role in various health conditions, including irritable bowel syndrome, anxiety, depression, and even neurological disorders like Parkinson's and Alzheimer's. Mayer also discusses the impact of lifestyle factors, such as diet, stress, and sleep, on the gut microbiome and how these factors can either promote or disrupt the delicate balance of this complex ecosystem.

"The Mind-Gut Connection" is a groundbreaking work that sheds light on the intricate communication network between our minds and our guts. It offers valuable insights into how we can optimize our gut health to improve our mental and physical well-being. By understanding this connection, we can make informed choices about our diet, lifestyle, and even our mental and emotional health, leading to a happier and healthier life. (The mind-gut connection, with Faith Dickerson, PhD, and Emeran Mayer, MD www.apa.org, The Mind-Gut Connection: How the Hidden Conversation Within Our Bodies Impacts Our Mood, Our Choices, and Our Overall Health - Amazon.com www.amazon.com, Bacteria in the gut have a direct line to the brain - News - The Rockefeller University www.rockefeller.edu)

While "The Mind-Gut Connection" by Dr. Emeran Mayer and "The Garden Within" by Dr. Anita Phillips approach the topic of holistic well-being from slightly different angles, they share a common thread: the profound interconnectedness of our inner worlds and their influence on our overall health. Mayer focuses primarily on the scientific underpinnings of the mind-gut connection, while Phillips delves into the emotional and spiritual dimensions, particularly for Black women. However, both authors emphasize the importance of nurturing our inner ecosystem, whether it be the gut microbiome or the emotional landscape, to achieve optimal health and healing.

Mayer's work provides a robust scientific framework for understanding how the gut microbiome, a complex community of microorganisms residing in our intestines, communicates with the brain. He explains the neural, hormonal, and immune pathways that link these two seemingly disparate systems, demonstrating how gut health can significantly impact mental and emotional well-being. He highlights the role of diet, stress, and lifestyle in shaping the microbiome and its influence on conditions ranging from irritable bowel syndrome to anxiety and depression. In essence, Mayer's research underscores the biological reality of the mind-body connection, emphasizing the gut as a key player in this intricate dance.

Phillips, in "The Garden Within," explores the inner landscape of Black women, recognizing the unique stressors and traumas they often face. She uses the metaphor of a garden to represent the inner self, emphasizing the importance of cultivating and tending to the emotional and spiritual roots. While not explicitly focusing on the gut microbiome, her work resonates with Mayer's findings by emphasizing the importance of nurturing the inner ecosystem. Phillips' "garden" encompasses emotional, psychological, and spiritual well-being, all of which are deeply intertwined with physical health. She advocates for self-care practices, emotional processing, and spiritual connection as essential tools for healing and resilience.

The correlation between the two works lies in their shared emphasis on the interconnectedness of our inner world and our overall well-being. Mayer's research provides the scientific basis for understanding how the gut, a vital part of our inner ecosystem, influences our mental and emotional states. Phillips' work complements this by exploring the emotional and spiritual dimensions of this inner world, particularly within the context of Black women's experiences. Both authors, in their respective domains, advocate for a holistic approach to health, recognizing that true well-being requires nurturing both the physical and the non-physical aspects of our being.

In conclusion, while "The Mind-Gut Connection" and "The Garden Within" approach the topic of holistic well-being from different perspectives, they converge on the fundamental principle of interconnectedness. Mayer's scientific exploration of the mind-gut axis provides a biological foundation for understanding how our inner ecosystem influences our health, while Phillips' focus on the emotional and spiritual landscape adds another layer of depth to this understanding. Together, these works offer a compelling case for the importance of nurturing our inner world, whether it be the gut microbiome or the emotional garden, as a pathway to optimal health, healing, and resilience. (Everything is connected: the link between mood & food - Mighty Pursuitmightypursuit.com, How Dr. Anita Phillips Cultivates “The Garden Within” - Apple Podcastspodcasts.apple.com, Five Things I Learned about Emotional Wellbeing from Dr Anita Phillips | by Isioma Ononye isiomanononye.medium.com)

My perspective on my breast cancer diagnosis shifted. I began to see it differently, almost as a calling. From my pain and fear, I discovered a renewed passion for life and a new way to connect with others. I love meeting new people. It helps to transform negative experiences into positive ones. There's always something good; you just have to change your perspective. Life presents us with opportunities. Situations arise, and it's up to us whether we let them define us or find the good within them. It's all about mindset. Your outlook determines the outcome. How you think shapes how you live. Notice I used the word "live"—an action word. You with breast cancer, you shall live. You with the failing kidney, you shall live. Will you leave a legacy for those who didn't make it?

Expectation

You Down with OPE?

Hell, nawh not ME!!! Other people's expectations or, better yet, OPE. Other people's perception. It boggles my mind sometimes how another person views a situation truly impacts how they act and think which dictates what they say out of their mouth. I have encountered a myriad of reactions to my diagnosis. The reaction to my infirmity ranges from pity to my favorite comment, "Look on the bright side…at least you get a free boob job!" It is that type of thinking that pisses me off, especially when the person is wrong.

I'm beyond frustrated with people underestimating the difficulty of dealing with breast cancer. I'm so tired of the assumptions and the way people go about their lives as if I'm fine. My reality changes day to day, and I almost feel guilty about it, just like I did during my first cancer experience. Things are different now because I've accepted my diagnosis and know miracles still happen. My perspective has shifted this second time around, but it still bothers me that people don't understand what living with breast cancer is like

Cancer isn't a one-size-fits-all situation; it's deeply personal and specific. Let me give you an example. The other day, I was trying to add my husband's credit card to my UberEats account. It was incredibly frustrating going through all the steps. My son saw my puffy, watery eyes and asked what I needed. When I explained, he gently took my phone, asked for my passcode, and added his father's card. I was so grateful. I just couldn't do it. It was frustrating and embarrassing, and I felt ashamed. He just said, "It's all good, Mom," and went on his way. Do you see how something as simple as adding a credit card became a monumental task that almost overwhelmed me? That's what I'm talking about. That's why I wrote this book. If it helps even one person understand, I'll have done my job.

My brother and I recently went on vacation together. We were sitting down outside the house and he brought back a memory of a fight where I was defending him. Remember I said that I do not like a situation where a person is at a disadvantage, and the perpetrator was wrong? The day before this incident happened, my brother was jumped and beaten. The guys that jumped on him actually had the wrong person. They were looking for a whole 'nother dude! This guy smacked my brother in the face with a textbook. As they began fighting, his friends jumped in. My brother is the only boy between my mother and my stepfather. He has six sisters. I am the oldest from my mom. I feel like my siblings are my responsibility. I am not going to allow someone to harm them, especially without retribution. That is how I was raised to take care of my brother and sisters as if I were mom. The next day, I gathered up about 10 of my girlfriends. We went down to University City High School for let out. The group of guys was nowhere to be found, but word spread fast. They knew that I was looking for them, all of them however put their hands on my brother. Whoever touched him. That's who I was looking for. You know how it is when the fight is about to happen. All the people that wanted to watch were instigating and giving information to the boys I wanted to fight. It just so happens that all the 'friends' who were there to assist in the jumping managed to get past me. However, the main guy who started to fight with my brother had jumped on the trolley trying to escape. Once I found out that the guy I wanted was on the trolley, I rallied my group and proceeded to walk toward 36th Street. The crowd that followed started to build and grow. The crowd started to take on a life of its own. The surge and the press of eager, agitated bodies propelled girls and me forward toward the trolley car. Fervent whispers, "He's on the trolley. " erupted and peppered my head, ears, and thoughts. This ninja thinks he is getting away…hmph! Not TODAY.

SEPTA trolleys in the 90s had an Emergency pull line outside at the back of the vehicle. I could see the boy looking out the window nervously as the crowd converged on the now-moving trolley. You know how crowds converge on and follow the action. This one was no different. The trolley paused for a moment Before pulling off. It really could not. I took that opportunity to pull the emergency line. This results in the trolley immediately stopping and the doors opening in the front and the back. I boarded the trolling with about three of my girls and confronted him. At first, he tried to act like he didn't know what I was talking about, but by the time I stopped the trolley, My brother was there, and he confirmed that this was indeed the one who had hit him with the book. There was nothing more to be said, We dragged him off of the trolley, and I kicked his ass. This was yet another example of a GIANT defeated, although he didn't seem that big when he was by himself. It's funny because whenever someone discusses this particular fight they always want to put emphasis on the fact that it was girls defending a boy. There is never a place for violence, but war happens.

The GIANT in this situation was injustice. Injustice is defined as a lack of fairness, an undeserved outcome, an unjust act or occurrence, or judging a person unfairly. When they attacked my brother, they not only acted as judge and jury, but they also delivered and carried out their own sentence. They expected to do this without consequences…they were wrong. I have a problem with situations like this, where other people's expectations are imposed on my life. Your expectations don't dictate my actions. This holds true even now that cancer has attacked me. I feel like my brother in this situation, like saying, "You've got the wrong person." I never bothered anyone. I was just minding my own business, and then, wham!

Now, I am expected to act a certain way. I am expected to look a certain way. I am expected to do certain things because I am a certain age. I am expected to feel a certain way because that's the normal response. Is that not an undeserved outcome? Cancer patient's outcomes in healing are tied to someone else's expectations? When you see it in black and white, the concept sounds ridiculous, but in most cancer-affected households, it is a reality. Cancer has caused me to realize myself as an individual. A collaboration of memories has joined together to help me in this time of crisis. Memories that have now forged a foundation from which I can battle. I am familiar with these war tactics and this particular GIANT.

The injustice of cancer is that it can kill you, and I think I can safely speak for my counterparts and say that we surely didn't ask for it. How unfair is that? I personally don't even have any type of history in my family. This just came out of nowhere. Imagine lying down finally to sleep after a long day of treatment, not sure how you are going to wake up the next morning. You don't know how you're going to feel. You don't know which part of your body is going to hurt the most. I am just happy to wake up in the morning. I could have been a statistic. Approximately 40,000 women die in the United States from breast cancer each year. I could have been one of those numbers. However, I am still here. You can not fathom the limitations that I face with this disease, and because you can't imagine what I go through on a daily basis, neither can most. I am still here. I would appreciate it if other people would keep their expectations of me to themselves and just let me heal the best way I see fit. I am still here. There is a part in Marvel Comics Madame Web where the main character's mother tells the doctor that she refuses to accept a diagnosis of helplessness. I feel the exact same way, and because of that, I am still here. Hey, Did I mention that I was still here?

The next GIANT I want to tackle is ANGER other people's and yours. Looking back on raising my children I encountered anger at an early age with my oldest son. I can remember a day when he got in trouble for destroying his room. I remember the day clearly because I used to get really bad migraine headaches in my 20s. The children were set up and trained to put in a video tape and sit quietly and watch TV in their room until Mommy woke up from her nap. I know it's not the best plan to sleep with children in the household with a bad headache, but my mom was downstairs on the first floor, and we lived on the third. The children also knew that they could go downstairs and get Grandma if anything was to really go wrong. I awoke to a carpet full of 20 oz worth of Cocoa Pebbles in the bedroom and the kitchen floor full of Comet cleanser. Suspect footprints between child and Cat were up and down the hallway and deer in headlights stares are all what received from the inhabitants of my household. I almost lost my mind. My mother said she could hear me hitting my note all the way downstairs on the first floor and, as usual, thanks for saving the kid because she was on her way upstairs to assess the situation. She sent me downstairs to her bed, shut the door quietly behind me, and proceeded to vacuum up the kid's bedroom and sweep up the kitchen floor was not a word. I was shot because I just knew I was going to go to jail that day. Coming out of a headache with not one expectation that my house would be a wreck almost sent me over the edge. Can you see how I felt about my cancer diagnosis? I said that day I did exactly what the Bible said to do. I was angry, but I did not sin that day. I said that the kids are still living. They've grown behind adults to this day. I even have grandchildren. I love me some Skylar and Zhaire! I love my Glam Babies! That was my anger welling up inside of me. You see, anger starts off as an ember. It's almost like a fire, and it grows into a GIANT and the key to dealing with and defeating this particular GIANT is to cut it off at the legs so that it doesn't grow into an uncontrollable beast. It’s because you feel like you have no control over the situation.

Soon after that incident, I ran into anger again, this time with my oldest son. He was home one afternoon and flat-out refused to do his homework. He was being really disrespectful and argumentative. So, I told him to get his stuff together and go outside. He went to get his shoes and shirt, but I told him to go out in what he was wearing—basketball shorts and a t-shirt. I told him he could come back in when he'd calmed down.

I sent him and his sister out as a way to build solidarity between them. It's a bond I have with my own siblings, and it's incredibly strong. I love seeing that kind of unbreakable love and loyalty in my kids, rather than them constantly fighting. So, yeah, when he went out, she had to go too. Not without protest, of course, because she's always the rational one, trying to understand why her brother feels the need to push my buttons.

You could hear them arguing as they went down the steps from our third-floor apartment to the front porch. She was trying to rationalize his anger and tantrums. It sounded like a therapy session, with their little voices pleading their cases about why they were on the porch and who should be apologizing. The look my son gave me as he walked past was pure anger. I don't care if it was coming from a 5-year-old or a 55-year-old. That was anger.

Now, even in my cancer journey, I've seen it again—in other people's eyes and in my own. It's a GIANT that needs to be dealt with. It can't be ignored and allowed to fester. It needs to be confronted and resolved. I read that internalized anger can turn into anxiety and depression, and I definitely don't need any more of that.

My condition already comes with its own set of challenges. I also read that anger and stress negatively impact healing, not just for cancer patients but for everyone. Your body doesn't heal when it's stressed. So, I wanted to examine these "GIANTS" and how they relate to my cancer journey, hoping it might help you on your journey, too.

Anger in a 5-year-old can manifest in a variety of ways, often appearing as a whirlwind of emotions and behaviors that can be both challenging and, at times, surprisingly insightful. It's important to remember that at this age, children are still developing their emotional regulation skills, and their expressions of anger can be more raw and unfiltered than those of older children or adults. Understanding the typical ways anger presents itself in a 5-year-old can help parents and caregivers respond with empathy and guidance.

One of the most common displays of anger in a 5-year-old is the classic tantrum. This might involve crying, screaming, kicking, hitting, or throwing objects. These outbursts can seem dramatic and overwhelming, but they often represent the child's frustration at not being able to articulate their needs or get what they want. A 5-year-old might throw themselves on the floor, pound their fists, or hold their breath until they turn red. These physical manifestations of anger are a way for them to release pent-up emotions when their verbal skills are not yet sufficient.

Beyond the dramatic displays of tantrums, anger can also manifest in more subtle ways. A 5-year-old might become withdrawn and quiet, refusing to speak or engage with others. They might sulk, pout, or give the "silent treatment." This withdrawal can be just as indicative of anger as an outward explosion. It can be a way for the child to express their displeasure and create distance from the perceived source of their frustration.

Aggression, both physical and verbal, is another common expression of anger at this age. A 5-year-old might hit, bite, or push other children or adults. They might also use hurtful words or name-calling. This aggression can be a way for them to assert their power and control in a situation where they feel powerless. It's important to address these aggressive behaviors firmly but calmly, helping the child understand that these actions are not acceptable.

Facial expressions and body language can also provide clues to a 5-year-old's anger. A furrowed brow, clenched fists, a tight jaw, and a red face are all common signs of rising anger. They might stomp their feet, cross their arms, or turn their back on someone. Paying attention to these nonverbal cues can help parents and caregivers recognize when a child is becoming angry before the situation escalates.

It's crucial to remember that anger in a 5-year-old is often a sign of unmet needs. They might be feeling tired, hungry, frustrated, or overwhelmed. They might be struggling with a developmental challenge or experiencing a change in their routine. By understanding the underlying causes of their anger, parents and caregivers can help them develop healthier coping mechanisms.

In conclusion, anger in a 5-year-old can take many forms, from dramatic tantrums to quiet withdrawal. It's important to view these expressions of anger as a normal part of development and to respond with patience, empathy, and understanding. By helping children learn to identify and manage their anger in healthy ways, we can equip them with essential emotional skills that will serve them well throughout their lives. (Should I Worry About My 5-Year-Old's Tantrums? | Little Otter Blog, www.littleotterhealth.com)(Temper Tantrums (for Parents) | Nemours KidsHealth kids health.org)(Does Your Child Have Tantrums? Should You Be Worried? > News > Yale Medicine www.yalemedicine.org)

Not all GIANTS are loud and boisterous. Some I believe, go unnoticed but continue in the background, a troubling undercurrent of chatter and little actions. IGNORANCE is one of those. You know, when you break a limb such as a leg or an arm, and you have a cast on as you are healing, other people can see physically that you are impaired. But when you have an intangible diagnosis such as cancer, nobody can really tell that you are impaired or that you're feeling sick that day. Maybe even if you're just not up to it, you don't have the energy to do the things that you used to do. Sometimes, this is the first GIANT people encounter because folks just plain don’t know. It’s not like I walk around with a banner saying Hey, I got breast cancer. I do wear a lot of t-shirts now that I think about it, smile. Insensitive people exist in regular life. You should be able to set your own pace and path. However, what I am not up for is what other people expect that I should be able to do. Having cancer is so personal, so individually different your difficulties are specific to you. The things that you need to do, although some may be similar, are specific to you, and no one has the right to decide, choose, or have an opinion as to what you should or should not be doing. This includes your medical professionals. They should be supplying the most up to date information for YOU to make your most informed decisions. Don't forget the family members who should be offering support rather than opinions in the same manner unless they are in charge of your care.

Let me give you an example. After my diagnosis and surgery, I met a doctor—let's call him Dr. So-and-So—who was supposed to be my oncologist. He terrified me. Being new to all this, I had questions about chemotherapy, its impact on someone of my ethnicity, and intimacy (since I'm married). He was completely unempathetic, and his staff was just as bad. He gave me generic answers, dismissing my concerns by saying his experience with other patients was sufficient, and then pawned off my other question to his nurse. As a new patient, I needed clear answers and some reassurance. I wanted someone to comfort me and tell me things would be okay.

The treatment he recommended was extensive and could have permanently damaged my heart and kidneys. To add insult to injury, when I went to find the nurse, she'd already left for the day. The remaining staff member, who was supposed to schedule my appointment with a cardiologist, gave me a disdainful look and remarked that no one would answer the phone at that hour, implying I should have known better. I sent my husband to the car, anticipating a confrontation. I told her to call me when she'd scheduled the appointment and left, feeling completely unheard and with new fears looming. I had no intention of returning to that office for treatment.

I left quickly and sought care at Fox Chase Cancer Center. Even with a recurrence, I continue to receive excellent care there. Fox Chase has patient advocates and social workers on staff, focused entirely on patient care. If you have any trouble getting your needs met, there are ways to address it. I hope this is true for all cancer centers and hospitals treating cancer because it's absolutely essential. We need to feel like we're our oncologist's only patient. This doctor assumed his bedside manner was acceptable and that I'd return for treatment. He was wrong on both counts. You can have numerous degrees and specialties but still be ignorant and invalidate them all. That's the truth.

Now, back to other people's expectations, the biggest violation of this is when it comes to energy and what you are up to do, what you need assistance with, and what you simply need to start saying no to. I go exclusively by the rule if I do not feel like it, I do not do it. I do not care what you all think about it. This is the time to focus on yourself, be selfish, and maybe even a bit of a “B” word. Your cancer journey is yours. You control the script, characters, location, and storyline. Don't let anyone take that from you. It's okay to have people help and make sure they care about you and what you want and wish for. If you are having problems keeping track of what those wants and wishes are, write them down. Don't hesitate to seek some assistance with this, if you need help with developing or organizing your ideas. It's OK to want what you want right now. It helps you heal and be resilient. Keep in mind that this time affects all aspects of you, your mental, physical, and spiritual well-being. All of them need healing.

When it comes to other people's expectations, I believe it often stems from arrogance. Like the doctor example, you'd be surprised how many people suddenly become "experts," offering unsolicited advice on everything from your daily fiber intake to every other aspect of your life. Frankly, it's incredibly irritating.

I believe attempting to control another person is a form of manipulation. Manipulation is defined as influencing someone in a clever or unscrupulous way—essentially, being dishonest and unfair, lacking moral principles. It's exploiting a relationship for personal gain. Someone dealing with cancer simply doesn't have the energy to focus on anyone else's needs. All their resources must be directed toward healing. No one should dictate your daily reality. Every day you wake up is a chance to share yourself with the world. When you open your eyes and feel that life-giving essence flowing through you, despite any aches or illness, you are alive.

The other day I woke up and I was so disoriented. I did not know what day it was, what time it was, it was really bad. It is an eerie feeling, to say the least. It is as if time stops, and everything stands still around you. Your mind is grabbing at the data that it's being given but it's just not computing into something that makes sense. What day is it? Where am I? What should I be doing right now? What time is it? I think the fact that I slept too close to 1:00 that day contributed to me being "off." I had slept right through breakfast, my morning meds and Price is Right. As I stood there bewildered, my husband answered the peppering of questions I was shooting at him. I couldn't help but wonder if anybody else went through this quirky scenario on weekends. I was nervous like I missed work or forgot to pick a kid up from school. Did I go all Freaky Friday…what …is… Happening!!!

The subtle clues of irritation with you in others are not obvious or blatant. You would not notice them immediately. These indications of annoyance are more like a barely audible sigh or a side sneer or roll of the eyes when they think you have looked elsewhere because you are taking longer than usual to make up your mind. What do I want to eat for dinner? There are so many factors to weigh that a usual person doesn't. First, am I even hungry? Second, what is going to taste good enough to get it down and keep it down, assuming that I will be able to taste it at all? And Third…What was I doing again? Damn Chemo Brain! These subtle never fully obvious signs of irritation can come as curt remarks with a tinge of impatience as if you intentionally meant to hold up any process. My favorite is the frustrated walk-off because I'm not catching your point or connecting the storyline. It used to bother me greatly when someone else was frustrated with me. I thought of the times when I was frustrated trying to relay my point, and I don't get upset so much anymore. It is hard to control someone else and to think that you can control someone else's thought process is even more impossible. Irrational even. You have to be comfortable enough to move on and not let it stress you. There will be a lot of these times where you will feel lost, disconnected, not present and it's ok. It is fleeting and comes and goes. Leave that conversation for another day. Healing is the focus, and comfort not only physically but comfort in who you are and where you are is key on any given subject. Nobody is 100%, 100% of the time. It is just that cancer patients are less than 100%, a little bit more than others.

To give you a sense of the cognitive challenges I've faced, I'll share an experience that illustrates the disorientation I've sometimes felt. A few months ago, I got out of bed in a dark room for a quick trip to the bathroom. Instead, I fell, hitting my head on the edge of my nightstand. It resulted in a lot of bleeding and a noticeable scar. Though I felt fine, just a little embarrassed and with a bruised ego, my medical team was concerned and ordered PET scans to check for internal injuries.

This incident prompted me to make some changes for my safety and comfort. I took the opportunity to declutter and create a "peace corner" in my room. The nightstand? Gone! This little nook is where I'm writing this book. It's my personal space within my bedroom, separate from where I sleep or nap (that's for the bed) and separate from where I work (that's for my chair). It’s important to have a dedicated space where you can be alone with your thoughts, a place to decompress after a long day of treatment or tests. Somewhere, you can relax, watch a show, and simply be. And if you get sleepy, you can easily get up and go to your bed for proper rest. Rest is essential.

Let me reiterate: you will be different after this. Cancer, its treatment, and its aftermath affect your mind, body, and spirit. Another common area of adjustment involves work. As I mentioned, some breast cancer treatments can cause side effects like difficulty focusing, slowed decision-making, confused thoughts, and memory problems.

Here's a key piece of advice: If you have the opportunity to take time off for treatment, including radiation or chemotherapy, please do it. I tried to be a superwoman, maintaining a full-time job, raising a teenager, attending church regularly, and fulfilling my roles as a wife, sister, and daughter—all the things I did before my diagnosis. My mindset was that cancer wouldn't defeat me. But this isn't about Joyce's experience; it's about yours. So, please, leave your superwoman cape at the door. You don't need it here. At this moment, the most important thing is to appreciate the miracle of being here, alive, and reading this book. Amen?

Try this: Inhale deeply, hold for four seconds, then exhale slowly through pursed lips for four seconds, making a "shhh" sound. Hold again for four seconds. Repeat this breathing exercise as many times as needed until you feel calm and peaceful.

Let me reiterate: you will be different after this. Cancer, its treatment, and its aftermath affect your mind, body, and spirit. Another common area of adjustment involves work. As I mentioned, some breast cancer treatments can cause side effects like difficulty focusing, slowed decision-making, confused thoughts, and memory problems.

Here's a key piece of advice: If you have the opportunity to take time off for treatment, including radiation or chemotherapy, please do it. I tried to be a superwoman, maintaining a full-time job, raising a teenager, attending church regularly, and fulfilling my roles as a wife, sister, and daughter—all the things I did before my diagnosis. My mindset was that cancer wouldn't defeat me. But this isn't about Joyce's experience; it's about yours. So, please, leave your superwoman cape at the door. You don't need it here. At this moment, the most important thing is to appreciate the miracle of being here, alive, and reading this book. Amen?

You don't know what tomorrow will bring. Rest in your miracle of being here, being in the present, the NOW, and being yourself. You are a blessing and a testimony because there are those who have gone home from breast cancer and are not alive right now. May they rest in peace. You are meant to read this. This conviction motivates me to be more than a patient and soon to be a survivor. I want to share the miraculous light within with other patients like me.

I learned this little trick in dealing with another GIANT … anger. Anger sneaks up on you. Very rarely can a person say I just jumped from a peaceful, calm state to instantly angry. I don't believe that it happens that way. I believe that anger starts out as a little flame, burning inside you right in the middle, close to the heart. That flame grows and intensity as the trigger feeds data to the mind that elicits this emotion. It just grows and grows in intensity, which results in an outburst. I'm so angry at cancer. I mean, who invited this disease into my life?! Certainly, I did not. I'm mad because it poses a threat to my longevity. It puts a question mark on my future memories. It is one of the greatest hiccups I have ever experienced in my life. I was not prepared for it, but I can say that my life experience has strengthened me for it.

The Mind

Have you ever been in a situation that was overwhelming, something that blindsided you, caught you totally unaware? That is how I feel about breast cancer. I don't believe anyone prepares themselves for the disasters that occur in our lives, not to the extent they really impact us. These times of uncertainty and desperation steer us to look for answers, solutions, and remedies. The difference is this time I can collect all the information for the answers. However, someone other than myself, a professional, is going to have to take the reins. I literally have turned my life over to others to sustain it. How about that? For trust? Remember how I spoke on emotions throughout this battle? I've had to address different thoughts, changing them from bad to good to have a positive effect on my health. It's called renewing your mind. Ephesians 4:23 says, instead, renew the thinking in your mind by the Spirit first, and clothe yourself with the new person created according to God's image. Notice it says God's image, not your pastor's, your deacon's, your mama's, your spouse's, or your bestie's … God's image. That's the trick. That's the tip. If you can renew your mind by the transformation of your heart to God, your healing is one of the greatest side effects, the best being eternal life and salvation. I actually used to tell the story like I found God. That would only be true if I were looking. I was not. I went to church to fight, to be honest, that Sunday. Yes, I know. I said fight. I remember exactly what I had worn. A suede fuchsia miniskirt with a white sweater. It had white fuchsia and lime green pearls, white stockings, and lime green penny loafers. My mother went back to a church where she attended as an usher. My godfather was an Associate Minister there. Of course, the ladies were on him. An unmarried minister in a Christian church is like having the chance to marry Barack Obama or LeBron James. Any who there was this woman who shall remain nameless. We will call her sister Watermelon. Now from what I understand, this lady would do things like snatch the collection plate from my mom or bumped into her for no reason, you know, petty stuff. Now, my mom is a petite woman. Little "SassaFras," a 5ft woman with a hearty soul full of joy, salt and pepper flowing hair, and cappuccino brown skin. This is a turn the other cheek, pray for your enemy, type of woman. She now has a grandmother-like quality that everybody just loves. That keeps us saying, "Who 'dis woman Harpo?" So you understand why this woman has to be respected and protected at all times. So, I decided to take vengeance into my own hands and confront this one. I mean, just who the hell do you think you are? I got my daughter for the weekend for further camouflage of my intentions. We arrived at church, and one time, I sat in the back, so I went to use the parishioners for my authority. My mom was an usher at this time, so I could see her in plain view. It was really easy to pick this woman out of the crowd. Church wasn't a cathedral building, more of a storefront deal. You know, close, intimate, it was time for offering. I watched each row stand up and walk forward, and Sister Watermelon came out of her row. Sure enough, she bumped the crap out of my mother. I stood up and moved my seat to the end of the row. She came back to her seat. And it's customary to either stand up or step out to let people back into their pew or to tuck your legs under and scooch back so they can pass the same way you do in a movie theater. That's what you're supposed to do in church. When Sister Watermelon came back to her seat, I didn't move. I actually stretched out my legs and stared at her straight in the eyes as she stepped over me to get to her seat. I continued looking her straight in her face until my mom must have picked up on the exchange and pinched me. She sent me back to my seat. I stared that lady in her eyes all the way back to my seat until I was sitting down. I say to myself, "I'm gonna see this heifer after church." My mom brought her change back to her in the offering plate, but she still snatched the contents out of the plate. The speaker of the hour was the Bishop of the church, and she spoke on forgiveness and allowing the Lord to fight your battles. She talked about temperance and payback and just how God could handle your battles better than you ever could. This woman was all about my business. I felt like she was talking directly to me. I was pissed that my mom had told this preacher all of the thoughts that I had, but how could that be? I got baptized around 10 years old, so I knew about the Holy Spirit, how he was supposed to be a comforter, and how he reveals things to people. I also knew that sometimes the ladies from down south in my church would get happy and catch the Holy Ghost and throw their wigs off. However, I never had a personal experience myself. I thought there was some type of conversation or gossip that my mom had participated in that I must have missed. The words the Bishop said cut through me like a knife and what in the world was this new feeling? I felt that before, but not in this context. Was I really ashamed of what I was thinking? Why in the world would I care about who knew my thoughts? Then a voice said, me, who? Voice me. God, I am God. I just put my head down because surely God wasn't talking to me. (Not me back here plotting to beat this lady up in the middle of altar call). Who in the world would know what I was thinking? I had not said a word to anyone about my plans. How does someone know enough? About Me? And what I was plotting). My attention was drawn to the word. That seizure. It was selling in my voice. It sounded in my brain. I heard it over and over again. God sees you. I have fought in church before. Right in the middle of the altar call, I smacked the bejesus out of this chick. But this time was different. I saw it felt something warm and comforting, like there was no need for me to strike out; thoughts of violence seemed to have melted away. Imagine waking up on a sunny Sunday winter morning. rays of sunlight splashing across the kitchen counter. As you push the start button on your favorite morning brew. You take a deep breath, looking out the window, and the warm light falls on your face instinctively; you lift your head up and breathe in that moment. It's that instant, that long connection. It felt like God, I felt God, I was standing at my kitchen counter drinking coffee. It was such an overtake and peace. I didn't have a care in the world. As the preacher continues to speak. She made comments like "Let it go." and "Put it in God's hands." Then, towards the end, she opened the doors of the church. This is when you invite people to join your church as members. I remember hearing, I got you as I got up to walk to the front of the altar. This was usually my time to strike, But I wasn't focused on getting Sister Watermelon anymore. I wanted more of that good morning feeling. That good morning feeling was GOD. I had my very own and had no clue what that was until I accepted Christ and joined the church that day. Into my heart, Accept his love that set the stage to stand on and fight breast cancer again today.

Maybe not that specific night, but very soon afterward, I woke up to a ceiling full of bluish-white floating fish-looking things. They covered my ceiling and sort of moved in a swimming session. They looked like skate fish, except they glowed brightly from the inside out like a fluorescent light bulb. They move gracefully in concert with each other. Fins flapping, moving smoothly, calmly smooth their individual spaces in the air, gliding effortlessly as in water. I asked God what I was looking at, and the word Sarafem dropped into my spirit. Now, Sarafem is a class of angelic beings. They have the highest order. They are light, and they have six wings. They fly around the throne in the throne room, crying to God. Holy, holy, holy Sarafem worships God continually. They minister to him and serve as agents of purification. There are six sets of wings because one set of their wings is for flying. One set is to cover their face and the last set covers their feet. You'll find the description of a Sarafem in Isaiah 6:1-3. The name comes from the Hebrew word Surat (meaning fire; we want the way they light.) They lit up my ceiling, and my bedroom was definitely illuminating and radiant, burning with an intense love of God. In that same instant, I felt warm, loved, held, seen, noticed, and cared about.

What do you think about when you are just sitting around thinking thoughts? Where does your mind wander when you allow it to just walk through the ideas that bubble up and pop up in your head? Is that place a good place? or is that a place of fear, doubt, or Terror? In the quiet times, the alone times, those just by yourself times, the parts of the day or the still of the night, where does your mind go? I will be honest: the first time I battled cancer, my mindset was to get it over with as quickly as possible. So I could get back to my quote unquote normal life. I responded so well to treatment I saw right into and through radiation. (This all occurred within one year after my diagnosis. I finished my last radiation treatment on 5-26-2022, And I was diagnosed back on May 25, 2021. I mean, who wouldn't want a testimony like that? God healed me in a year from breast cancer; in August of 2022, CT scans showed that the cancer had come back. Clear was no case. I actually hung their report on my desk. I was so proud. You couldn't find a prep at my table question in my mind about how real God is. You know, I never did get to jump on Sister Watermelon that day. Something clicked just like something clicked when the cancer came back.

After about a week of sulking and feeling sorry for myself I was wondering what I did wrong to make it come back, just like the first time, sometimes it just happens. In my case, the cells mutated. I looked to see what good had come of what I considered a mess of a situation. I have lost four family members since I'd been diagnosed with cancer. That hit so close to home. I was medicated through most of the home going services, and even so, it was tough. I hang on because if I wake up daily, there must be something for me to do here on this Earth. It could be something as simple as writing this book. Now that I think about it, I have never laid down for a challenge. I usually defend the underdog, and in this whole situation with cancer, I am the underdog.

My mind thinks all kinds of thoughts when I'm just sitting thinking. Now that I no longer work I find myself with more time on my hands and think about what to do with it. I don't want to waste it because, to be honest, it's borrowed. Nothing is promised, especially tomorrow. So what do you think about when you're a cancer patient going through all kinds of therapies and sessions and things to keep you alive? I tend to think about the things that I have accomplished. I think back on all the ideas that I had in my thirties, failed Pursuits, missed opportunities and I wonder if I could ever get them back. That's what cancer changed about me. I savor each day, every moment. I feel like Anything is Possible if I wake up in the morning. It is that thought process that got me started writing this book. Cancer is not an end-all diagnosis, and yes, I think this even for ones with a terminal diagnosis. What can you do today that you thought about yesterday? What can you do to work towards something that you want to accomplish? Every day, I try to accomplish one task that will move forward an idea or goal I want to do.

I started by getting a journal and listing my goals. My top three were: 1) write this book, 2) keep all my health appointments, and 3) lose 20 pounds. I have this habit of writing everything in my journal—prayers, ideas, hopes, wishes—believing it will all come to pass. I added to it daily until a week before I sent it to the publisher.

Would you believe that cancer patients actually miss and cancel appointments? One morning, while answering phones for dispatch triage, a young woman called in, crying openly as she gave me her information. I asked if she was okay. Through her tears, she explained she had an important corporate meeting and couldn't make her follow-up appointment for her cancer diagnosis. I could see her biopsy results and knew what she'd be discussing. I couldn't break confidentiality, but I gently persuaded her to move her meeting to the afternoon so she could see her doctor that morning. It was crucial she got that information.

That kind of thing happened often—people calling to cancel appointments because of other pressing issues. I was usually able to convince them that their health was more important. My focus was to get them into the office so they could address their health needs.

I think we don't prioritize self-care enough these days. We push forward, putting aside our health for less important tasks. I made it a point to attend every appointment for test results, scans, treatments, and everything. When you have cancer, these things—treatments and follow-ups—are vital. Nothing is more important than your health.

I'm Not Done Yet

Cancer made me feel hopeless, alone, and helpless. It made me anxious and scared. But I fought it once, and now I see it differently. It has made me stronger and more willing to share. It has made me more grateful for humanity. It has made me more hopeful and faithful to God. It has made me more amazed by God and His grace. Many others have died from breast cancer, but I'm still here. (Even though it has come back and spread to my lung.) I have a different outlook on life. I don't want to sit in the background and just heal anymore. I've already done that once. Now, it's time for me to act. This is the end of this book, but not the end of my journey. I will not stop slaying GIANTS. I will continue to conquer those big obstacles and things that I think are larger than life in my world. However, the difference is now I want to take all of you along with me.

Courage is strength in your heart to do what is right in the face of fear. Pastor Michael Todd says in his Damaged but Not Destroyed series that you never want to give up in the middle of the miracle. He says when traumatic things happen to us, they tend to rob us of our faith, our hope, and our "try." You don't want the damage that cancer has done or caused to hold you in place. However, it has been stated that I will battle cancer forever. I choose to focus on the fact that I will be cancer-free soon and look forward to remission. Overcoming and slaying your GIANTS starts in your mind. Let's just address the elephant in the room. I, like you, am fearful of dying. Remember how I said earlier you had to look at things differently. Cancer is one of those things.

It's funny. One of the biggest challenges I've faced is that writing this book while being semi-retired and healing has given me a lot of time and space to think. I initially thought the book would just pour out of me, that I'd be completely consumed by it. But it didn't happen that way. Instead, it came in bits and pieces—passages, stories, memories, bursts of ideas that made me say, "Oh yeah, I remember that." It came from reliving anxious moments and remembering past hurts and offenses. It came from moments of loneliness and abandonment, from which sprang hope and faith. It came from utter terror and chaos, yet also from a place of complete peace, tranquility, and rest. It came from bright mornings and dark nights, from moonlit skies and overwhelmingly bright days. It was a mix, a collaboration of thoughts, memories, and ideas, all tied together by this one breast cancer diagnosis. Everything converged in this one spot. My life. My health. My motherhood. My sisterhood. My daughterhood. My grand daughterhood. My grand motherhood. All of these titles were challenged, not even including auntie, niece, half-sister, stepsister, sister, and girlfriend…sheesh!

Looking ahead to my future living with breast cancer, I've been thinking about what I can control. I envision a future where breast cancer patients have access to tailored, specific services. I see every patient having at least one person to accompany them to doctor's visits and provide support. Just one person to be there when they're scared and nervous, someone to talk to during all the poking and prodding. I imagine paid companions and cancer-specific life coaches available to every patient, regardless of race, gender, lifestyle, or background. Quality, affordable services where the only requirement is a breast cancer diagnosis. And I want to see these services expand to other cancers, like prostate and lung.

Every single one of us deserves a companion at chemotherapy and radiation sessions. Even doctor's visits to discuss test results can be daunting and require someone to hold our hand if needed. It bothers me to see people sitting alone. I usually try to strike up a conversation just to bring a smile to their face. It's a testament to Fox Chase Cancer Center that everyone there, from the maintenance staff to the doctors, always has a smile. Everyone is so personable; it's amazing. I carry that with me as I go out into the world. I'm smiling because, honestly, I didn't have to be here. Keep that in mind. A breast cancer diagnosis can bring about a wide range of emotional challenges. It's common to experience a mix of feelings, including shock, fear, anger, sadness, and uncertainty. These emotions can be intense and may fluctuate throughout the course of diagnosis, treatment, and beyond.

Many individuals diagnosed with breast cancer find themselves grappling with a sense of loss. This might involve the loss of a sense of normalcy, control over their bodies, or even changes in their physical appearance due to surgery or treatment. These losses can be difficult to process and may lead to feelings of grief and sadness.

Anxiety and fear are also common emotional responses. Concerns about the future, the effectiveness of treatment, and the possibility of recurrence can weigh heavily on the mind. These worries can sometimes lead to difficulty sleeping, concentrating, or making decisions.

It's important to acknowledge and validate these emotions. There is no right or wrong way to feel, and everyone's experience is unique. Seeking support from loved ones, support groups, or mental health professionals can be incredibly beneficial in navigating these emotional challenges. Remember, you don't have to go through this alone. (Coping with breast cancer emotionally breastcancernow.org, Emotional stages of a breast cancer diagnosis | LBBC www.lbbc.org, Emotions and Cancer – NCI www.cancer.govind)

Battling breast cancer is a challenging journey, but many women successfully overcome the disease. Here's some comprehensive approach tips that are helping in my success. DO NOT REPLACE SOUND MEDICAL ADVICE:

1. Early Detection is Key:

2. Regular Screenings: Follow recommended guidelines for mammograms, clinical breast exams, and self-exams. Early detection significantly improves treatment outcomes.

3. Know Your Risk Factors: Discuss your family history and any concerns with your doctor to determine your risk level and screening schedule.

4. Seek Expert Medical Care:

5. Find a Multidisciplinary Team: Look for a team of specialists including surgeons, oncologists, radiation oncologists, and other healthcare professionals experienced in breast cancer treatment.

6. Get Multiple Opinions: Don't hesitate to seek second or third opinions to ensure you're comfortable with your treatment plan.

7. Understand Your Diagnosis:

8. Know Your Cancer Type: Learn about the specific type of breast cancer you have, it's stage, and any hormone receptor or HER2 status.

9. Ask Questions: Don't hesitate to ask your medical team about anything you don't understand. Knowledge is power.

10. Explore Treatment Options:

11. Surgery: Options include lumpectomy, mastectomy, or lymph node removal. Discuss the benefits and risks of each with your surgeon.

12. Radiation Therapy: Uses high-energy rays to kill cancer cells.

13. Chemotherapy: Uses drugs to destroy cancer cells, often used for more aggressive cancers.

14. Hormone Therapy: Blocks or lowers hormones that fuel cancer growth, used for hormone receptor-positive cancers.

15. Targeted Therapy: Attacks specific vulnerabilities in cancer cells, often used for HER2-positive cancers.

16. Immunotherapy: Helps your immune system fight cancer cells.

17. Clinical Trials: Consider participating in clinical trials to access the latest treatments and contribute to research.

18. Maintain a Healthy Weight: Being overweight increases breast cancer risk and recurrence.

19. Eat a Balanced Diet: Focus on fruits, vegetables, whole grains, and lean protein. Limit processed foods, red meat, and sugary drinks.

20. Exercise Regularly: Aim for at least 30 minutes of moderate-intensity exercise most days of the week.

21. Limit Alcohol: Excessive alcohol consumption increases breast cancer risk.

22. Don't Smoke: Smoking is harmful to overall health and can increase cancer risk.

23. Build a Strong Support System:

24. Connect with Others: Join support groups or online communities to share experiences and find encouragement.

25. Seek Emotional Support: Talk to a therapist, counselor, or trusted friend or family member.

26. Lean on Your Loved Ones: Allow friends and family to help with practical tasks and provide emotional support.

27. Stay Positive and Hopeful:

28. Focus on the Present: Take each day as it comes and celebrate small victories.

29. Practice Mindfulness: Meditation and relaxation techniques can help manage stress and anxiety.

30. Believe in Yourself: Remember that you are strong and resilient.

31. Follow Your Treatment Plan:

32. Attend All Appointments: Keep all scheduled appointments and follow your medical team's recommendations.

33. Communicate with Your Team: Report any side effects or concerns promptly.

34. Embrace Survivorship:

35. Follow-Up Care: after treatment, follow your doctor's recommendations for regular checkups and screenings.

36. Adjust to Life after Treatment: Be patient with yourself as you adjust to physical and emotional changes.

37. Live a Full and Meaningful Life: Focus on your passions, relationships, and overall well-being.

Remember: Every breast cancer journey is unique. There is no one-size-fits-all approach. Work closely with your medical team to develop a personalized treatment plan that's right for you.

INVITATION

Come On in the Water's fine.

Life can often feel like a winding road filled with unexpected turns, challenging climbs, and confusing detours. We search for meaning, for purpose, for something that anchors us amidst the storms. In this search, many have found solace, hope, and unwavering love in a relationship with Jesus Christ.

Perhaps you've heard the stories, the parables, the teachings. Maybe you've witnessed the transformative power of faith in the lives of others. Or perhaps you're simply curious, wondering if there's more to this story than you've understood.

This is a gentle invitation to explore. To consider the possibility that there is a love that surpasses all understanding, a grace that forgives all shortcomings, and a hope that transcends any circumstance. This invitation isn't about judgment or condemnation; it's about opening your heart to the possibility of a profound and personal connection.

Jesus Christ offered himself as a bridge between humanity and God, a way to find forgiveness, healing, and eternal life. It's a path that's been walked by millions across centuries, each with its unique story of encountering divine love.

There's no pressure, no obligation, just an open door. Consider exploring the scriptures, talking to someone you trust about faith, or simply spending some quiet time in reflection. If you feel a stirring in your heart, a sense of longing or curiosity, perhaps it's an invitation you're meant to accept. The journey of faith is a personal one, and it begins with a single step. Perhaps today is the day to take yours. Stephanie Ike Oka for prayed a prayer that caught my attention while I was writing the conclusion. It came from her YouTube video called You've Got Something on the One channel. During her prayer, she said something like. Right now, heavenly father, we love you who is like you, Lord Jesus. You know that your love is what transforms us from the inside out, and I thank you, Lord, that your sons and daughters would know that you were never about keeping anything from them but that you want to work something in them that they would begin to be like you. They would be transformed into your image and bear the fruits that speak of you. Lord, I pray you would equip them, equip them with their fruits, and then send them into the marketplace so the world can see y ou are a healing and loving God. A God that moves in boldness. Allow the reader of this word confidence that they would move to know that heaven is backing them up as they submit to you and stand against the GIANTS in their lives. Have your way, Holy Ghost, as we face this infirmity.

Heal Lord. Send Your Comforter God. Move in the lives of your sons and daughters, and Lord, let it be our testimony.

Help us change this world for the Kingdom of God. I surrender my will to yours this day. I believe that you are my Savior, Jesus. I am Yours. In Jesus' name, we pray. Amen

As I mentioned at the beginning, I'm not one to push my beliefs on anyone. I truly believe what's meant for you will find you. If anything I've shared has resonated with you, I want to give you the chance to find the same answers I found. Why would I keep something like this to myself? Psalm 34:19 says, "Many are the afflictions of the righteous, but the Lord delivers us out of them all." Where else can you find an answer to "Why me?" when facing something like cancer? I'm not saying God gave you cancer to bring you closer to him, but I am saying He will walk through it with you when no one else is there. If you're at a point where you feel lost and don't know where to turn, say these simple words aloud, if you can: "Lord, I pray that everyone reading these words realizes that you have the answers, the promise of peace. We know you didn't say we'd be without affliction or pressure. I confess that you are my Lord and Savior, crucified for my sins. Just as you rose, free and victorious, I rise with you. Today, we thank you for being by our side and withholding no good thing. I confess that, through ignorance, I may not have known where to turn. But today, I come against ignorance. I come against doubt and fear. I come against guilt and shame. I come against hurt and pain."

God, thank you for loving us so much that you gave us your only son so that he could die so I could live. I accept Jesus as my savior today at this moment. I believe Jesus died on the cross and rose again on the third day. We invite the Holy Spirit into our hearts. Lead us and guide us in your ways, Lord. May your will be done in my life. In Jesus Name, Amen.

Listen, aside from all the spiritual stuff, I don't want you to close this book still feeling like you are alone in this cancer battle. I want you to understand that you have a sister in your cause. I want you to understand that at least one other person knows how you feel when you're up sick at night or in the morning, for that matter. I want you to understand that at least one other person knows how it feels to get poked and prodded with all kinds of tests and measurements. I want you to understand that at least one other person knows the fear that you feel when you hear that "C" word. I want you to understand that at least one other person understands what it feels like to gather your thoughts to properly express how you're feeling. I need you to understand that I feel you I really do, and I'm praying all good things for you. We got this. We truly do.

In the end, the battle against the Goliath of breast cancer is a deeply personal one. Each individual, like David facing his GIANT, must find their own sling and stone, their own source of strength and resilience. Whether it's the unwavering support of loved ones, the cutting-edge advancements of medical science, or an unshakeable faith in the power of the human spirit, the tools for victory are out there. This book has explored the many facets of this fight, from the initial shock of diagnosis to the long road of treatment and recovery. But more than that, it has sought to illuminate the courage, the determination, and the hope that reside within each person facing this challenge. Remember, even in the face of seemingly insurmountable odds, the human spirit has an extraordinary capacity to endure, to adapt, and ultimately, to triumph. The journey may be arduous, but you are not alone, and the fight is never over.

So, that's our journey through the world of breast cancer. It's been a lot, right? From diagnosis to treatment and beyond, it's a rollercoaster. But one thing's for sure: you're stronger than you think. Whether you're a patient, a survivor, or a support person, remember that every experience is valid, and there's no one "right" way to navigate this. Take what you need from this book, leave the rest, and know that there's a whole community out there cheering you on every step of the way. You've got this. I fought like a wild cat coming up. I always rooted for the underdog. I don't consider anyone a stray. We were equals even though no one else wanted to be or even noticed. I feel the same way about cancer. It’s a bully attacking the most feminine representation of a woman: her curves. As a result, the woman is impacted in mind, body, and soul. I pray that something in here helps you overcome your Goliaths. I pray God’s will, in Jesus' name, grace and blessings over your life. Remember, you don’t have breast cancer. You are fighting breast cancer. Do Not accept it for what it is. Now get outta here and go…SLAY!

Notes and Resources

A

- American Cancer Society. (2024). *Understanding Breast Cancer*. Retrieved from www.cancer.org

B

- Breastcancer.org. (2024). *Chemotherapy Side Effects.* Retrieved from www.breastcancer.org

C

- Centers for Disease Control and Prevention (CDC). (2024). *Genetic Testing for Hereditary Breast and Ovarian Cancer.* Retrieved from www.cdc.gov
  Charlotte Radiology. (2024). *Understanding BRCA Gene Testing for Breast and Ovarian Cancer Risk.* Retrieved from www.charlotteradiology.com

H

- Healthline. (2024). *How to Protect Your Kidneys During Chemotherapy.* Retrieved from www.healthline.com

- Healthline. (2024). *Retinal Bleeding: Symptoms, Causes, Diagnosis, and Treatment.* Retrieved from www.healthline.com
- Holy Bible App. www.bible.com

M

- Mount Sinai - New York. (2024). *High Blood Pressure and Eye Disease Information.* Retrieved from www.mountsinai.org

N

- National Cancer Institute (NCI). (2024). *BRCA Gene Changes: Cancer Risk and Genetic Testing Fact Sheet.* Retrieved from www.cancer.gov
- National Cancer Institute (NCI). (2024). *Constipation and Cancer - Side Effects.* Retrieved from www.cancer.gov

P

- PubMed Central (PMC). (2024). *Pain Associated with Breast Cancer: Etiologies and Therapies.* Retrieved from www.ncbi.nlm.nih.gov

- PubMed Central (PMC). (2024). *The Relationship Between Father Absence and Hostility Among Chinese Depressed Youths.* Retrieved from www.ncbi.nlm.nih.gov

S

- StatPearls - NCBI Bookshelf. (2024). *Hypertensive Retinopathy.* Retrieved from www.ncbi.nlm.nih.gov

T

- The American Heart Association. (2024). *How High Blood Pressure Can Lead to Vision Loss.* Retrieved from www.heart.org

W

- World Health Organization (WHO). (2024). *Cancer and Global Health Statistics.* Retrieved from www.who.int

Made in the USA
Columbia, SC
08 April 2025